Directions

Theodore Clymer
Leo Ruth
Peter Evanechko
Julia Higgs

CONSULTANTS
Roger W. Shuy • Linguistics
E. Paul Torrance • Creativity

GINN AND COMPANY
A XEROX EDUCATION COMPANY

ACKNOWLEDGMENTS

Grateful acknowledgment is made to the following authors and publishers for permission to use copyrighted materials:

Delacorte Press for "Gee, You're So Beautiful That It's Starting to Rain." From *The Pill Versus the Springhill Mine Disaster* by Richard Brautigan. Copyright © 1968 by Richard Brautigan. A Seymour Lawrence Book/Delacorte Press. Reprinted by permission of the publisher.

E. P. Dutton & Co., Inc., for *"from* A Precocious Autobiography." From the book *A Precocious Autobiography* by Yevgeny Yevtushenko. Trans. by Andrew R. MacAndrew. Copyright © 1963 by E. P. Dutton & Co., Inc. and used with their permission.

Farrar, Straus & Giroux, Inc., for "Bad Characters" by Jean Stafford. Reprinted with the permission of Farrar, Straus & Giroux, Inc. from *Collected Stories* by Jean Stafford, copyright © 1954, 1969 by Jean Stafford.

Harper & Row, Publishers, Inc., for "John Pappas Tries Out for the Mets" from *Assignment: Sports* by Robert M. Lipsyte. Copyright © 1970 by Robert M. Lipsyte. Reprinted by permission of Harper & Row Publishers. Also for "At the Aquarium" from *Poems of Five Decades* by Max Eastman. Copyright, 1954 by Max Eastman. Also for "Fifteen" from *The Rescued Year* by William Stafford. Copyright © 1964 by William Stafford. Both reprinted by permission of Harper & Row, Publishers, Inc.

Random House, Inc., for "I'm of Siberian Stock" by Yevgeny Yevtushenko. From *Two Centuries of Russian Verse*, edited by Avrahm Yarmolinsky. Copyright 1949, © 1962, 1965 by Avrahm Yarmolinsky. Reprinted by permission of Random House, Inc.

Mrs. Katherine Birmingham for "Don't Bother with the Ants" by William Birmingham. Copyright 1955, by Fire Island Publishing Corporation. Reprinted with permission of Mrs. Katherine Birmingham.

Jonathan Cape Ltd, London, for "Gee, You're So Beautiful That It's Starting to Rain" from *The Pill Versus the Springhill Mine Disaster* by Richard Brautigan. Reprinted by permission of Jonathan Cape Ltd.

Collins Publishers, London, for the excerpt from *A Precocious Autobiography* by Yevgeny Yevtushenko. Used with permission of Collins Publishers.

Cowles Syndicate for "How To Win At Basketball: Cheat" by Bill Cosby. Appeared originally in the January 27, 1970, issue of *Look* Magazine. Reprinted with permission of Cowles Syndicate.

Mrs. Edgar Lee Masters for "Lucinda Matlock" from *A Spoon River Anthology* by Edgar Lee Masters. Reprinted by permission.

University of Notre Dame Press for "In the Barrio," adapted from *Barrio Boy* by Ernesto Galarza. Reprinted by permission of University of Notre Dame Press.

Murray Pollinger, London, in association with James Brown Associates, for "Bad Characters" by Jean Stafford, from *Collected Stories of Jean Stafford*. Copyright © 1954, 1969 by Jean Stafford. Published in England by Chatto & Windus Ltd., London. Reprinted by permission of Murray Pollinger.

Theron Raines for "John Pappas Tries Out for the Mets" from *Assignment: Sports* by Robert M. Lipsyte. Copyright © 1970 by Robert M. Lipsyte. Reprinted by permission of Theron Raines.

Rod Serling for his play "A Storm in Summer," produced originally by the National Broadcasting Company, Inc. Permission to reprint granted by Rod Serling. No performance of the play may be given without authorization.

2

The Swallow Press, Inc., for "Joyrider" by James Schevill. Reprinted from *Violence and Glory: Poems 1962-1968* © 1969 by permission of The Swallow Press, Chicago.

John Williams for "The Skaters" from *The Necessary Lie*, copyright 1965 by John Williams. Used by permission of the author.

Graphic Design by James Pfeufer Associates, Inc.

Acknowledgment is made to the following for art and photography on the pages indicated:

Kathy Anderson, 18, 27; David Bell, 42-43; Reed Champion (cover design), 8; Laurence Channing, 12; Bob Combs, 72; Bill Finch, 4-5, 48-49; Christopher G. Knight, 47; Rita Faye Landis, 64; Metromedia, 84, 86, 104, 117; Marc Riboud/Magnum, 17; Wide World, 56.

At the Aquarium

Serene the silver fishes glide,
Stern-lipped, and pale, and wonder-eyed!
As through the aged deeps of ocean,
They glide with wan and wavy motion!
They have no pathway where they go.
They flow like water to and fro.
They watch with never-winking eyes,
They watch with staring, cold surprise,
The level people in the air,
The people peering, peering there:
Who also wander to and fro,
And know not why or where they go,
Yet have a wonder in their eyes,
Sometimes a pale and cold surprise.

Max Eastman

Contents

Don't Bother with the Ants

Last week I took my family off on a long-promised trip to the mountains. Our departure posed certain problems, which, in one way or another, are probably roughly similar to those experienced by any family which includes an eight-year-old boy.

A kindly neighbor dug out the following letter from his files. He said that it had been written to him in circumstances much the same as ours and he felt reasonably sure that if he again followed the instructions contained in the letter, he could solve most of our problems. This he did and the results were so successful that I am reprinting it here for the benefit of anybody who may be confronted with the same situation.

Dear Harry,
Wonder if you would take care of Bob's farm while we are away?
(1) Main thing is the turtles. Every once in a while you sprinkle dried bugs in their water for them to eat. A can of these bugs is usually next to the turtle bowl or under Bob's pillow.

(2) About the spiders. If you happen to catch a fly you might throw it in the mason jar. Personally, I wouldn't unscrew the top for anything. They seem to multiply rapidly and in a pinch, will get along eating each other.

(3) Bob's green caterpillars were taken off his tomato plants because they were chewing up the leaves. The only thing they will eat is tomato leaves. So if you feel as sorry for them as Bob does, tear off the top of the tomato plants once in a while and feed them. Personally, I wouldn't unscrew that jar either.

(4) I don't think it will be necessary to pull up the carrots every day to see how they are coming along, but I know that is part of the farming method used by Bob and it seems to stimulate the carrots... Ditto, the radishes.

(5) As far as the ants are concerned, don't bother with them. The holes in the top of the jar are for ventilation, and for some reason unfathomable to us, the ants seem to stay contained.

(6) The baby-food carton that makes the scratching noises has got a praying mantis inside. I don't know the plural of mantis, but I do know that the contents of the carton are plural. There are at least three hundred of them, in fact, and I suppose something

ought to be done. Bob raised them from
something brown and hard he brought in
from the back yard and he says they will
eat all the harmful bugs in the garden. For
reasons best known to himself and the mantis
-- and the other two hundred and ninety-nine
-- he is reluctant to release them. Any disposal
thoughts you may have on this will be
considered mighty neighborly.

(7) The polliwogs. If you will go in the
rear bathroom you will notice that the tub
is full of water and that there are a lot of
things swimming around. We gave Bob
permission to do this in the interests of
expediency. Fact is, he wouldn't leave until
he knew they were under cover. Since they
have gotten to be a sensitive subject around
here, I am not inclined to ask him what
they eat. If you can find out anywheres
I wish you would throw them some.

(8) Last thought: If you come upon
anything in the general neighborhood
of his room that moves, will you please
put it back in a mason jar. Then throw
in some dried bugs, tomato leaves and
carrots and screw the top on hard.

Many, many thanks.
Fred

from A Precocious Autobiography

"I wanted to conquer my fear of Red.
So I wrote a poem about him."

In 1944 I was living alone in an empty apartment in a small quiet Moscow street, Chetvertaya Meshchanskaya.

My parents were divorced. My father was somewhere in Kazakhstan with his new wife and their two children. I seldom received letters from him.

My mother was at the front. She had given up her work as a geologist to become a singer and was giving concerts for the troops.

My education was left to the street. The street taught me to swear, smoke, spit elegantly through my teeth, and to keep my fists up, always ready for a fight—a habit which I have kept to this day.

The street taught me not to be afraid of anything or anyone—this is another habit I have kept.

I realized that what mattered in the struggle for existence was to overcome my fear of those who were stronger.

The ruler of our street, Chetvertaya Meshchanskaya, was a boy of about sixteen who was nicknamed Red.

Red's shoulders were incredibly broad for a boy of his age.

Red walked masterfully up and down our street, his legs wide apart and with a slightly rolling gait, like a seaman on the deck of his ship.

From under his peaked cap, always worn back to front, his forelock tumbled down in a fiery cascade, and out of his round pockmarked face, green eyes, like a cat's, sparkled with scorn for everything and everyone crossing his path. Two or three lieutenants, in peaked caps back to front like Red's, trotted at his heels.

Red could stop any boy and say impressively the one word "money." His lieutenants would turn out the boy's pockets, and if he resisted they gave him a real beating.

Everyone was afraid of Red. I too was afraid. I knew he carried heavy brass knuckles in his pocket.

I wanted to conquer my fear of Red.

So I wrote a poem about him.

This was my first piece of journalism in verse.

By the next day the whole street knew the piece by heart and relished it with triumphant hatred.

One morning on my way to school I suddenly came upon Red and his lieutenants. His eyes seemed to bore through me. "Ah, the poet," he drawled, smiling crookedly. "So you write verses. Do they rhyme?"

Red's hand darted into his pockets and came out with its brass knuckles; it flashed like lightning and struck my head. I fell down streaming with blood and lost consciousness.

This was my first payment as a poet.

I spent several days in bed.

When I went out, with my head still bandaged, I again saw Red. I struggled with instinctive fear but lost and took my heels.

I ran all the way home. There I rolled on my bed, biting my pillow and pounding it with my fists in shame and impotent fury at my cowardice.

But then I made up my mind to vanquish it at whatever cost.

14

I went into training with parallel bars and weights, and after every session I would feel my muscles. They were getting harder, but slowly. Then I remembered something I had read in a book about a miraculous Japanese method of wrestling which gave an advantage to the weak over the strong. I sacrificed a week's ration card for a textbook on jujitsu.

For three weeks I hardly left home—I trained with two other boys. Finally I felt I was ready and went out.

Red was sitting on the lawn in our yard, playing Twenty-one with his lieutenants. He was absorbed in the game.

Fear was still in me and it ordered me to turn back. But I went up to the players and kicked the cards aside with my foot.

Red looked up, surprised at my impudence after my recent flight.

He got up slowly. "You looking for more?" he asked menacingly.

As before, his hand dived into his pocket for the brass knuckles. But I made a quick jabbing movement, and Red, howling with pain, rolled on the ground. Bewildered, he got up and came at me, swinging his head furiously from side to side like a bull.

I caught his wrist and squeezed slowly, as I had read in the book, until the brass knuckles dropped from his limp fingers. Nursing his hand, Red fell down again. He was sobbing and smearing the tears over his pockmarked face with his grimy fist. His lieutenants discreetly withdrew.

That day Red ceased to rule our street.

And from that day on I knew for certain that there is no need to fear the strong. All one needs is to know the method of overcoming them. There is a special jujitsu for every strong man.

What I also learned that day was that, if I wished to be a poet, I must not only write poems but also know how to stand up for what I have written.

Yevgeny Yevtushenko

☐ What effect does the poem have upon Red? How does it affect the other boys on the street? How does Yevgeny defeat Red?

☐ What do you think Yevgeny means when he says, "There is a special jujitsu for every strong man"?

☐ What does this autobiographical account reveal about Yevgeny's attitude toward life?

☐ In his sketch Yevgeny shows great courage when he decides to defeat the bully. Read his poem "I'm of Siberian Stock" on page 17. What are some of the forces that shaped Yevgeny's character?

■ ■

■ In this excerpt from "A Precocious Autobiography," Yevgeny Yevtushenko describes an incident from his early school days. The poem "I'm of Siberian Stock" details some of the rigorous aspects of his life as a young worker. Make up a series of questions you would ask the poet if you were to interview him. Try to relate your questions to the aspect of his life you wish to know more about.

■ Yevtushenko recalls a time when he gained confidence in his ability to see through a bully like Red. In describing the incident, he uses direct, simple language to recreate for the reader the intense emotions he felt. Using a similar writing style, describe an incident in your own life in which you gained a certain self-respect. Try to make the reader feel the intensity of your emotions during this incident.

I'm of Siberian Stock

I'm of Siberian stock.
Wild garlic I ate with my bread,
and as a boy
            I towed
the ferry just like a man.
The cables were steel: my hands
were on fire.
A muscular fellow,
                    big-browed,
I was a riveter, and
with a shovel
            I dug
deep, where they told me to dig.
They didn't bawl me out,
didn't talk rot,
they put an ax in my hands,
like it or not, taught me to work.
And if they beat me when
the firewood I cut was no good,
they did as they should,
out of love, wishing me well.
I sweated blood,
bowed under a sack.
I worked with a scythe,
with chopper and pickax.
I fear nobody's lip;
there's no heartache I fear.
My hands are bruised,
my grip strong as a vise.
There's nothing in the world
that I don't dare. I grin
at an enemy,
because whatever it is, I'm fit,
I can handle it.

Yevgeny Yevtushenko

Bad Characters

*"It turned out that she did not know
how to play any games at all;
she couldn't do anything and didn't want
to do anything; her only recreation and
her only gift was, and always had been,
stealing."*

Up until I learned my lesson in a very bitter
way, I never had more than one friend at a time, and my
friendships, though ardent, were short. When they ended and I
was sent packing in unforgetting indignation, it was always
my fault; I would swear vilely in front of a girl I knew to be
pious and prim (by the time I was eight, the most grandilo-
quent gangster could have added nothing to my vocabulary—I
had an awful tongue), or I would call a Tenderfoot Scout a
sissy, or make fun of athletics to the daughter of the high
school coach. These outbursts came without plan; I would simply one day, in the middle of a game of Russian bank or a hike
or a conversation, be possessed with a passion to be by myself,
and my lips instantly and without warning would accommodate
me. My friend was never more surprised than I was when this
irrevocable slander, this terrible, talented invective, came boil-
ing out of my mouth.

Afterward, when I had got the solitude I had wanted, I
was dismayed, for I did not like it. Then I would sadly finish the
game of cards as if someone were still across the table from
me; I would sit down on the mesa and through a glaze of tears
would watch my friend departing with outraged strides;
mournfully, I would talk to myself. Because I had already al-

ienated everyone I knew, I then had nowhere to turn, so a famine set in and I would have no companion but Muff, the cat, who loathed all human beings except, significantly, me—truly. She bit and scratched the hands that fed her, she arched her back like a Halloween cat if someone kindly tried to pet her, she hissed, laid her ears flat to her skull, growled, fluffed up her tail into a great bush and flailed it like a bullwhack. But she purred for me, she patted me with her paws, keeping her claws in their velvet scabbards. She was not only an ill-natured cat, she was also badly dressed. She was a calico, and the distribution of her colors was a mess; she looked as if she had been left out in the rain and her paint had run. She had a Roman nose as the result of some early injury, her tail was skinny, she had a perfectly venomous look in her eye. My family said—my family discriminated against me—that I was much closer kin to Muff than I was to any of them. To tease me into a tantrum, my brother Jack and my sister Stella often called me Kitty instead of Emily. Little Tess did not dare, because she knew I'd chloroform her if she did. Jack, the meanest boy I have ever known in my life, called me Polecat and talked about my mania for fish, which, it so happened, I despised. The name would have been far more appropriate for *him*, since he trapped skunks up in the foothills—we lived in Adams, Colorado—and quite often, because he was careless and foolhardy, his clothes had to be buried, and even when that was done, he sometimes was sent home from school on the complaint of girls sitting next to him.

Along about Christmastime when I was eleven, I was making a snowman with Virgil Meade in his backyard, and all of a sudden, just as we had got around to the right arm, I had to be alone. So I called him a son of a sea cook, said it was common knowledge that his mother had bedbugs and that his father, a dentist and the deputy marshal, was a bootlegger on the side. For a moment, Virgil was too aghast to speak—a little earlier we had agreed to marry someday and become millionaires—and then, with a bellow of fury, he knocked me down and washed my face in the snow. I saw stars, and black balls bounced before my eyes. When finally he let me up, we were both crying, and he hollered that if I didn't get off his property that instant, his father would arrest me and send me to Canon

City. I trudged slowly home, half frozen, critically sick at heart. So it was old Muff again for me for quite some time. Old Muff, that is, until I met Lottie Jump, although "met" is a euphemism for the way I first encountered her.

I saw Lottie for the first time one afternoon in our own kitchen, stealing a chocolate cake. Stella and Jack had not come home from school yet—not having my difficult disposition, they were popular, and they were at their friends' houses, pulling taffy, I suppose, making popcorn balls, playing casino, having fun—and my mother had taken Tess with her to visit a friend in one of the T.B. sanitariums. I was alone in the house, and making a funny-looking Christmas card, although I had no one to send it to. When I heard someone in the kitchen, I thought it was Mother home early, and I went out to ask her why the green pine tree I had pasted on a square of red paper looked as if it were falling down. And there, instead of Mother and my baby sister, was this pale, conspicuous child in the act of lifting the glass cover from the devil's-food my mother had taken out of the oven an hour before and set on the plant shelf by the window. The child had her back to me, and when she heard my footfall, she wheeled with an amazing look of fear and hatred on her pinched and pasty face. Simultaneously, she put the cover over the cake again, and then she stood motionless as if she were under a spell.

I was scared, for I was not sure what was happening, and anyhow it gives you a turn to find a stranger in the kitchen in the middle of the afternoon, even if the stranger is only a skinny child in a moldy coat and sopping wet basketball shoes. Between us there was a lengthy silence, but there was a great deal of noise in the room: the alarm clock ticked smugly; the teakettle simmered patiently on the back of the stove; Muff, cross at having been waked up, thumped her tail against the side of the terrarium in the window where she had been sleeping—contrary to orders—among the geraniums. This went on, it seemed to me, for hours and hours while that tall, sickly girl and I confronted each other. When, after a long time, she did open her mouth, it was to tell a prodigious lie. "I came to see if you'd like to play with me," she said. I think she sighed and stole a sidelong and regretful glance at the cake.

Beggars cannot be choosers, and I had been missing Virgil so sorely, as well as all those other dear friends forever lost to me, that in spite of her flagrance (she had never clapped eyes on me before, she had had no way of knowing there was a creature of my age in the house—she had come in like a hobo to steal my mother's cake), I was flattered and consoled. I asked her name and, learning it, believed my ears no better than my eyes: Lottie Jump. What on earth! What on earth—you surely will agree with me—and yet when I told her mine, Emily Vanderpool, she laughed until she coughed and gasped. "Beg pardon," she said. "Names like them always hit my funny bone. There was this towhead boy in school named Delbert Saxonfield." I saw no connection and I was insulted (what's so funny about Vanderpool, I'd like to know), but Lottie Jump was, technically, my guest and I *was* lonesome, so I asked her, since she had spoken of playing with me, if she knew how to play Andy-I-Over. She said, "Naw." It turned out that she did not know how to play any games at all; she couldn't do anything and didn't want to do anything; her only recreation and her only gift was, and always had been, stealing. But this I did not know at the time.

As it happened, it was too cold and snowy to play outdoors that day anyhow, and after I had run through my list of indoor games and Lottie had shaken her head at all of them (when I spoke of Parcheesi, she went "Ugh!" and pretended to be sick), she suggested that we look through my mother's bureau drawers. This did not strike me as strange at all, for it was one of my favorite things to do, and I led the way to Mother's bedroom without a moment's hesitaton. I loved the smell of the lavender she kept in gauze bags among her chamois gloves and linen handkerchiefs and filmy scarves; there was a pink fascinator knitted of something as fine as spider's thread, and it made me go quite soft—I wasn't soft as a rule, I was as hard as nails and I gave my mother a rough time—to think of her wearing it around her head as she waltzed on the ice in the bygone days. We examined stockings, nightgowns, camisoles, strings of beads, and mosaic pins, keepsake buttons from dresses worn on memorial occasions, tortoiseshell combs, and a transformation made from Aunt Joey's hair when she had racily had it bobbed.

Lottie admired particularly a blue cloisonné perfume flask with ferns and peacocks on it. "Hey," she said, "this sure is cute. I like thing-daddies like this here." But very abruptly she got bored and said, "Let's talk instead. In the front room." I agreed, a little perplexed this time, because I had been about to show her a remarkable powder box that played *The Blue Danube*. We went into the parlor, where Lottie looked at her image in the pier glass for quite a while and with great absorption, as if she had never seen herself before. Then she moved over to the window seat and knelt on it, looking out at the front walk. She kept her hands in the pockets of her thin dark red coat; once she took out one of her dirty paws to rub her nose for a minute and I saw a bulge in that pocket, like a bunch of jackstones. I know now that it wasn't jackstones, it was my mother's perfume flask; I thought at the time her hands were cold and that that was why she kept them put away, for I had noticed that she had no mittens.

Lottie did most of the talking, and while she talked, she never once looked at me but kept her eyes fixed on the approach to our house. She told me that her family had come to Adams a month before from Muskogee, Oklahoma, where her father, before he got tuberculosis, had been a brakeman on the Frisco. Now they lived down by Arapahoe Creek, on the west side of town, in one of the cottages of a wretched settlement made up of people so poor and so sick—for in nearly every ramshackle house someone was coughing himself to death—that each time I went past I blushed with guilt because my shoes were sound and my coat was warm and I was well. I wished that Lottie had not told me where she lived, but she was not aware of any pathos in her family's situation, and, indeed, it was with a certain boastfulness that she told me her mother was the short-order cook at the Comanche Café (she pronounced this word in one syllable), which I knew was the dirtiest, darkest, smelliest place in town, patronized by coal miners who never washed their faces and sometimes had such dangerous fights after drinking dago red that the sheriff had to come. Laughing, Lottie told me that her mother was half Indian, and, laughing even harder, she said that her brother didn't have any brains and had never been to school. She herself was eleven years old, but she was only in the third grade, because teachers had always had it in for her—making her go to the blackboard and all like that when she was tired. She hated school—she went to Ashton, on North Hill, and that was why I had never seen her, for I went to Carlyle Hill—and she especially hated the teacher, Miss Cudahy, who had a head shaped like a pine cone and who had killed several people with her ruler. Lottie loved the movies ("Not them Western ones or the ones with apes in," she said. "Ones about hugging and kissing. I love it when they die in that big old soft bed with the curtains up top, and he comes in and says 'Don't leave me, Marguerite de la Mar' "), and she loved to ride in cars. She loved Mr. Goodbars, and if there was one thing she despised worse than another it was tapioca. ("Pa calls it fish eyes. He calls floating island horse spit. He's a big piece of cheese. I hate him.") She did not like cats (Muff was now sitting on the mantelpiece, glaring like an owl); she kind of liked snakes—except cottonmouths and rat- tlers—because she found them kind of funny; she had once seen a goat eat a tin can. She said that one of these days she would take me downtown—it was a slowpoke town, she said, a one-horse burg (I had never heard such gaudy, cynical talk and was trying to memorize it all)—if I would get some money for the trolley fare; she hated to walk, and I ought to be proud that she had walked all the way from Arapahoe Creek today for the sole solitary purpose of seeing me.

Seeing our freshly baked dessert in the window was a more likely story, but I did not care, for I was deeply impressed by this bold, sassy girl from Oklahoma and greatly admired the poise with which she aired her prejudices. Lottie Jump was certainly nothing to look at. She was tall and made of skin and bones; she was evilly ugly, and her clothes were a disgrace, not just ill-fitting and old and ragged but dirty, unmentionably so; clearly she did not wash much or brush her teeth, which were notched like a saw, and small and brown (it crossed my mind that perhaps she chewed tobacco); her long, lank hair looked as if it might have nits. But she had personality. She made me think of one of those self-contained dogs whose home is where his handout is and who travels alone but, if it suits him to, will become the leader of a pack. She was aloof, never looking at

24

me, but amiable in the way she kept calling me "kid." I liked her enormously, and presently I told her so.

At this, she turned around and smiled at me. Her smile was the smile of a jack-o'-lantern—high, wide, and handsome. When it was over, no trace of it remained. "Well, that's keen, kid, and I like you, too," she said in her downright Muskogee accent. She gave me a long, appraising look. Her eyes were the color of mud. "Listen, kid, how much do you like me?"

"I like you loads, Lottie," I said. "Better than anybody else, and I'm not kidding."

"You want to be pals?"

"Do I!" I cried. So *there*, Virgil Meade, you big fat hoot-nanny, I thought.

"All right, kid, we'll be pals." And she held out her hand for me to shake. I had to go and get it, for she did not alter her position on the window seat. It was a dry, cold hand, and the grip was severe, with more a feeling of bones in it than friendliness.

Lottie turned and scanned our path and scanned the sidewalk beyond, and then she said, in a lower voice, "Do you know how to lift?"

"Lift?" I wondered if she meant to lift *her*. I was sure I could do it, since she was so skinny, but I couldn't imagine why she would want me to.

"Shoplift, I mean. Like in the five-and-dime."

I did not know the term, and Lottie scowled at my stupidity.

"*Steal*, for crying in the beer!" she said impatiently. This she said so loudly that Muff jumped down from the mantel and left the room in contempt.

I was thrilled to death and shocked to pieces. "Stealing is a sin," I said. "You get put in jail for it."

"Ish ka bibble! I should worry if it's a sin or not," said Lottie, with a shrug. "And they'll never put a smart old whatsis like *me* in jail. It's fun, stealing is—it's a picnic. I'll teach you if you want to learn, kid." Shamelessly she winked at me and grinned again. (That grin! She could have taken it off her face and put it on the table.) And she added, "If you don't, we can't be pals, because lifting is the only kind of playing I like. I hate those dumb games like Statues. Kick-the-Can—phooey!"

I was torn between agitation (I went to Sunday school and knew already about morality; Judge Bay, a crabby old man who loved to punish sinners, was a friend of my father's and once had given Jack a lecture on the criminal mind when he came to call and found Jack looking up an answer in his arithmetic book) and excitement over the daring invitation to misconduct myself in so perilous a way. My life, on reflection, looked deadly prim; all I'd ever done to vary the monotony of it was to swear. I knew that Lottie Jump meant what she said—that I could have her friendship only on her terms (plainly, she had gone it alone for a long time and could go it alone for the rest of her life)—and although I trembled like an aspen and my heart went pitapat, I said, "I want to be pals with you, Lottie."

"All right, Vanderpool," said Lottie, and got off the window seat. "I wouldn't go braggin' about it if I was you. I wouldn't go telling my ma and pa and the next-door neighbor that you and Lottie Jump are going down to the five-and-dime next Saturday aft and lift us some nice rings and garters and things like that. I mean it, kid." And she drew the back of her forefinger across her throat and made a dire face.

"I won't. I promise I won't. My *gosh*, why would I?"

"That's the ticket," said Lottie, with a grin. "I'll meet you at the trolley shelter at two o'clock. You have the money. For both down and up. I ain't going to climb up that ornery hill after I've had my fun."

"Yes, Lottie," I said. Where was I going to get twenty cents? I was going to have to start stealing before she even taught me how. Lottie was facing the center of the room, but she had eyes in the back of her head, and she whirled around back to the window; my mother and Tess were turning in our front path.

"Back way," I whispered, and in a moment Lottie was gone; the swinging door that usually squeaked did not make a sound as she vanished through it. I listened and I never heard the back door open and close. Nor did I hear her, in a split second, lift the glass cover and remove that cake designed to feed six people.

I was restless and snappish between Wednesday afternoon and Saturday. When Mother found the cake was gone, she scolded me for not keeping my ears cocked. She assumed, naturally, that a tramp had taken it, for she knew I hadn't eaten it; I never ate anything if I could help it (except for raw potatoes, which I loved) and had been known as a problem feeder from the beginning of my life. At first it occurred to me to have a tantrum and bring her around to my point of view: my tantrums scared the living daylights out of her because my veins stood out and I turned blue and couldn't get my breath. But I rejected this for a more sensible plan. I said, "It just so happens I didn't hear anything. But if I had, I suppose you wish I had gone out in the kitchen and let the robber cut me up into a million little tiny pieces with his sword. You wouldn't even bury me. You'd just put me on the dump. *I* know who's wanted in this family and who isn't." Tears of sorrow, not of anger, came in powerful tides and I groped blindly to the bedroom I shared with Stella, where I lay on my bed and shook with big, silent *weltschmerzlich*[1] sobs. Mother followed me immediately, and so did Tess, and both of them comforted me and told me how much they loved me. I said they didn't; they said they did. Presently, I got a headache, as I always did when I cried, so I got to have an aspirin and a cold cloth on my head, and when Jack and Stella came home, they had to be quiet. I heard Jack say, "Emily Vanderpool is the biggest polecat in the U.S.A. Whyn't she go in the kitchen and say, 'Hands up'? He woulda lit out." And Mother said, "Sh-h-h! You don't want your sister to be sick, do you?" Muff, not realizing that Lottie had replaced her, came in and curled up at my thigh, purring lustily; I found myself glad that she had left the room before Lottie Jump made her proposition to me, and in gratitude I stroked her unattractive head.

Other things happened. Mother discovered the loss of her perfume flask and talked about nothing else at meals for two whole days. Luckily, it did not occur to her that it had been stolen—she simply thought she had mislaid it—but her monomania got on my father's nerves and he lashed out at her and at the rest of us. And because I was the cause of it all and my con-

---

[1] *weltschmerzlich* (velt′shmerts lik)

science was after me with red-hot pokers, I finally *had* to have a tantrum. I slammed my fork down in the middle of supper on the second day and yelled, "If you don't stop fighting, I'm going to kill myself. Yammer, yammer, nag, nag!" And I put my fingers in my ears and squeezed my eyes tight shut and screamed so the whole county could hear, "Shut *up!*" And then I lost my breath and began to turn blue. Daddy hastily apologized to everyone, and Mother said she was sorry for carrying on so about a trinket that had nothing but sentimental value—she was just vexed with herself for being careless, that was all, and she wasn't going to say another word about it.

I never heard so many references to stealing and cake, and even to Oklahoma (ordinarily no one mentioned Oklahoma once in a month of Sundays) and the ten-cent store as I did throughout those next days. I myself once made a ghastly slip and said something to Stella about "the five-and-dime." "The five-and-*dime!*" she exclaimed. "Where'd you get *that* kind of talk? Do you by any chance have reference to the *ten-cent store?*"

The worst of all was Friday night—the very night before I was to meet Lottie Jump—when Judge Bay came to play two-handed pinochle with Daddy. The Judge, a giant in intimidating haberdashery—for some reason, the white piping on his vest bespoke, for me, handcuffs and prison bars—and with an aura of disapproval for almost everything on earth except what pertained directly to himself, was telling Daddy, before they began their game, about the infamous vandalism that had been going on among the college students. "I have reason to believe that there are girls in this gang as well as boys," he said. "They ransack vacant houses and take everything. In one house on Pleasant Street, up there by the Catholic Church, there wasn't anything to take, so they took the kitchen sink. Wasn't a question of taking everything *but*—they took the kitchen sink."

"What ever would they want with a kitchen sink?" asked my mother.

"Mischief," replied the Judge. "If we ever catch them and if they come within my jurisdiction, I can tell you I will give them no quarter. A thief, in my opinion, is the lowest of the low."

Mother told about the chocolate cake. By now, the fiction was so factual in my mind that each time I thought of it I saw a funny-paper bum in baggy pants held up by rope, a hat with holes through which tufts of hair stuck up, shoes from which his toes protruded, a disreputable stubble on his face; he came up beneath the open window where the devil's-food was cooling and he stole it and hotfooted it for the woods, where his companion was frying a small fish in a beat-up skillet. It never crossed my mind any longer that Lottie Jump had hooked that delicious cake.

Judge Bay was properly impressed. "If you will steal a chocolate cake, if you will steal a kitchen sink, you will steal diamonds and money. The small child who pilfers a penny from his mother's pocketbook has started down a path that may lead him to holding up a bank."

It was a good thing I had no homework that night, for I could not possibly have concentrated. We were all sent to our rooms, because the pinochle players had to have absolute quiet. I spent the evening doing cross-stitch. I was making a bureau runner for a Christmas present; as in the case of the Christmas card, I had no one to give it to, but now I decided to give it to Lottie Jump's mother. Stella was reading *Black Beauty*, crying. It was an interminable evening. Stella went to bed first; I saw to that, because I didn't want her lying there awake listening to me talking in my sleep. Besides, I didn't want her to see me tearing open the cardboard box—the one in the shape of a church, which held my Christmas Sunday-school offering. Over the door of the church was this shaming legend: "My mite for the poor widow." When Stella had begun to grind her teeth in her first deep sleep, I took twenty cents away from the poor widow, whoever she was (the owner of the kitchen sink, no doubt), for the trolley fare, and secreted it and the remaining three pennies in the pocket of my middy. I wrapped the money well in a handkerchief and buttoned the pocket and hung my skirt over the middy. And then I tore the paper church into bits—the heavens opened and Judge Bay came toward me with a double-barrelled shotgun—and hid the bits under a pile of pajamas. I did not sleep one wink. Except that I must have, because of the stupendous nightmares that kept wrenching the flesh off my skeleton and caused me to come close to perishing of thirst; once I fell out of bed and hit my head on Stella's ice skates. I would have waked her up and given her a piece of my mind for leaving them in such a lousy place, but then I remembered: I wanted *no* commotion of any kind.

I couldn't eat breakfast and I couldn't eat lunch. Old Johnny-on-the-spot Jack kept saying, "*Poor* Polecat. Polecat wants her fish for dinner." Mother made an abortive attempt to take my temperature. And when all that hullabaloo subsided, I was nearly in the soup because Mother asked me to mind Tess while she went to the sanitarium to see Mrs. Rogers, who, all of a sudden, was too sick to have anyone but grownups near her. Stella couldn't stay with the baby, because she had to go to ballet, and Jack couldn't, because he had to go up to the mesa and empty his traps. ("No, they *can't* wait. You want my skins to rot in this hot-one-day-cold-the-next weather?") I was arguing and whining when the telephone rang. Mother went to answer it and came back with a look of great sadness; Mrs. Rogers, she had learned, had had another hemorrhage. So Mother would not be going to the sanitarium after all and I needn't stay with Tess.

By the time I left the house, I was as cross as a bear. I felt awful about the widow's mite and I felt awful for being mean about staying with Tess, for Mrs. Rogers was a kind old lady, in a cozy blue hug-me-tight and an old-fangled boudoir cap, dying here all alone; she was a friend of Grandma's and had lived just down the street from her in Missouri, and all in the world Mrs. Rogers wanted to do was go back home and lie down in her own big bedroom in her own big, high-ceilinged house and have Grandma and other members of the Eastern Star come in from time to time to say hello. But they wouldn't let her go home; they were going to kill or cure her. I could not help feeling that my hardness of heart and evil of intention had had a good deal to do with her new crisis; right at the very same minute I had been saying "Does that old Mrs. Methuselah *always* have to spoil my fun?" the poor wasted thing was probably coughing up her blood and saying to the nurse, "Tell Emily Vanderpool not to mind me, she can run and play."

I had a bad character, I know that, but my badness never gave me half the enjoyment Jack and Stella thought it did. A good deal of the time I wanted to eat lye. I was certainly having no fun now, thinking of Mrs. Rogers and of depriving that poor widow of bread and milk; what if this penniless woman without a husband had a dog to feed, too? Or a baby? And besides, I didn't want to go downtown to steal anything from the ten-cent store; I didn't want to see Lottie Jump again—not really, for I knew in my bones that that girl was trouble with a capital "T." And still, in our short meeting she had mesmerized me; I would think about her style of talking and the expert way she had made off with the perfume flask and the cake (how had she carried the cake through the streets without being noticed?) and be bowled over, for the part of me that did not love God was a black-hearted villain. And apart from these considerations, I had some sort of idea that if I did not keep my appointment with Lottie Jump, she would somehow get revenge; she had seemed a girl of purpose. So, revolted and fascinated, brave and lily-livered, I plodded along through the snow in my flopping galoshes up toward the Chautauqua, where the trolley stop was. On my way, I passed Virgil Meade's house; there was not just a snowman, there was a whole snow family in the backyard, and Virgil himself was throwing a stick for his dog. I was delighted to see that he was alone.

Lottie, who was sitting on a bench in the shelter eating a Mr. Goodbar, looked the same as she had the other time except that she was wearing an amazing hat. I think I had expected her to have a black handkerchief over the lower part of her face or to be wearing a Jesse James waistcoat. But I had never thought of a hat. It was felt; it was the color of cooked meat; it had some flowers appliquéd on the front of it; it had no brim, but rose straight up to a very considerable height, like a monument. It sat so low on her forehead and it was so tight that it looked, in a way, like part of her.

"How's every little thing, bub?" she said, licking her candy wrapper.

"Fine, Lottie," I said, freshly awed.

A silence fell. I drank some water from the drinking fountain, sat down, fastened my galoshes, and unfastened them again.

"My mother's teeth grow wrong way too," said Lottie, and showed me what she meant: the lower teeth were in front of the upper ones. "That so-called trolley car takes its own sweet time. This town is blah."

To save the honor of my home town, the trolley came scraping and groaning up the hill just then, its bell clanging with an idiotic frenzy, and ground to a stop. Its broad, proud cowcatcher was filled with dirty snow, in the middle of which rested a tomato can, put there, probably, by somebody who was bored to death and couldn't think of anything else to do—I did a lot of pointless things like that on lonesome Saturday afternoons. It was the custom of this trolley car, a rather mysterious one, to pause at the shelter for five minutes while the conductor, who was either Mr. Jansen or Mr. Peck, depending on whether it was the A.M. run or the P.M., got out and stretched and smoked and spit. Sometimes the passengers got out, too, acting like sightseers whose destination was this sturdy stucco gazebo instead of, as it really was, the Piggly Wiggly or the Nelson Dry. You expected them to take snapshots of the drinking fountain or of the Chautauqua meeting house up on the hill. And when they got back in the car, you expected them to exchange intelligent observations on the aborigines and the ruins they had seen.

Today there were no passengers, and as soon as Mr. Peck got out and began staring at the mountains as if he had never seen them before while he made himself a cigarette, Lottie, in her tall hat (was it something like the Inspector's hat in the Katzenjammer Kids?), got into the car, motioning me to follow. I put our nickels in the empty box and joined her on the very last double seat. It was only then that she mapped out the plan for the afternoon, in a low but still insouciant voice. The hat— she did not apologize for it, she simply referred to it as "my hat"—was to be the repository of whatever we stole. In the future, it would be advisable for me to have one like it. (How? Surely it was unique. The flowers, I saw on closer examination, were tulips, but they were blue, and a very unsettling shade of blue.) I was to engage a clerk on one side of the counter, asking her the price of, let's say, a tube of Daggett & Ramsdell vanishing cream, while Lottie would lift a round comb or a barrette or a hair net or whatever on the other side. Then, at a signal, I would decide against the vanishing cream and would move on to the next counter that she indicated. The signal was interesting; it was to be the raising of her hat from the rear— "like I've got the itch and gotta scratch," she said. I was relieved that I was to have no part in the actual stealing, and I was touched that Lottie, who was going to do all the work, said we would "go halvers" on the take. She asked me if there was anything in particular I wanted—she herself had nothing special in mind and was going to shop around first—and I said I would like some rubber gloves. This request was entirely spontaneous; I had never before in my life thought of rubber gloves in one way or another, but a psychologist—or Judge Bay— might have said that this was most significant and that I was planning at that moment to go on from petty larceny to bigger game, armed with a weapon on which I wished to leave no fingerprints.

On the way downtown, quite a few people got on the trolley, and they all gave us such peculiar looks that I was chicken-hearted until I realized it must be Lottie's hat they were looking at. No wonder. I kept looking at it myself out of the corner of my eye; it was like a watermelon standing on end. No, it was like a tremendous test tube. On this trip—a slow one, for the trolley pottered through that part of town in a desultory, neighborly way, even going into areas where no one lived— Lottie told me some of the things she had stolen in Muskogee and here in Adams. They included a white satin prayer book (think of it!), Mr. Goodbars by the thousands (she had probably never paid for a Mr. Goodbar in her life), a dinner ring valued at two dollars, a strawberry emery, several cans of corn, some shoelaces, a set of poker chips, countless pencils, four spark plugs ("Pa had this old car, see, and it was broke, so we took 'er to get fixed; I'll build me a radio with 'em sometime—you know? Listen in on them ear muffs to Tulsa?"), a Boy Scout knife, and a Girl Scout folding cup. She made a regular practice of going through the pockets of the coats in the cloakroom every day at recess, but she had never found anything there worth a red cent and was about to give that up. Once, she had taken a gold pencil from a teacher's desk and had got caught— she was sure that this was one of the reasons she was only in the third grade. Of this unjust experience, she said, "The old hoot owl! If I was drivin' in a car on a lonesome stretch and she was settin' beside me, I'd wait till we got to a pile of gravel and then I'd stop and say, 'Git out, Miss Priss.' She'd git out, all right."

Since Lottie was so frank, I was emboldened at last to ask her what she had done with the cake. She faced me with her grin; this grin, in combination with the hat, gave me a surprise from which I have never recovered. "I ate it up," she said. "I went in your garage and sat on your daddy's old tires and ate it. It was pretty good."

There were two ten-cent stores side by side in our town, Kresge's and Woolworth's, and as we walked down the main street toward them, Lottie played with a Yo-Yo. Since the street was thronged with Christmas shoppers and farmers in for Saturday, this was no ordinary accomplishment; all in all, Lottie Jump was someone to be reckoned with. I cannot say that I was proud to be seen with her; the fact is that I hoped I would not meet anyone I knew, and I thanked my lucky stars that Jack was up in the hills with his dead skunks because if he had seen her with that lid and that Yo-Yo, I would never have heard the last of it. But in another way I *was* proud to be with her; in a smaller hemisphere, in one that included only her and me, I was swaggering—I felt like Somebody, marching along beside this lofty Somebody from Oklahoma who was going to hold up the dime store.

There is nothing like Woolworth's at Christmastime. It smells of peanut brittle and terrible chocolate candy, Djer-Kiss talcum powder and Ben Hur Perfume—smells sourly of tinsel and waxily of artificial poinsettias. The crowds are made up largely of children and women, with here and there a deliberative old man; the women are buying ribbons and wrappings and Christmas cards, and the children are buying asbestos pot holders for their mothers and, for their fathers, suede bookmarks with a burnt-in design that says "A good book is a good friend" or "Souvenir from the Garden of the Gods." It is very noisy. The salesgirls are forever ringing their bells and asking the floorwalker to bring them change for a five; babies in go-carts are screaming as parcels fall on their heads; the women, waving rolls of red tissue paper, try to attract the attention of the harried girl behind the counter. ("Miss! All I want is this one batch of the red. Can't I just give you the dime?" And the girl, beside herself, mottled with vexation, cries back, "Has to be rung up, Moddom, that's the rule.") There is pandemonium at the toy counter, where things are being tested by the customers—wound up, set off, tooted, pounded, made to say "Maaaah-Maaaah!" There is very little gaiety in the scene and, in fact, those baffled old men look as if they were walking over their own dead bodies, but there is an atmosphere of carnival, nevertheless, and as soon as Lottie and I entered the doors of Woolworth's golden-and-vermilion bedlam, I grew giddy and hot—not pleasantly so. The feeling, indeed, was distinctly disagreeable, like the beginning of a stomach upset.

Lottie gave me a nudge and said softly, "Go look at the envelopes. I want some rubber bands."

This counter was relatively uncrowded (the seasonal stationery supplies—the Christmas cards and wrapping paper and stickers—were at a separate counter), and I went around to examine some very beautiful letter paper; it was pale pink and it had a border of roses all around it. The clerk here was a cheerful middle-aged woman wearing an apron, and she was giving all her attention to a seedy old man who could not make up his mind between mucilage and paste. "Take your time, Dad," she said. "Compared to the rest of the girls, I'm on my vacation." The old man, holding a tube in one hand and a bottle in the other, looked at her vaguely and said, "I want it for stamps. Sometimes I write a letter and stamp it and then don't mail it and steam the stamp off. Must have ninety cents' worth of stamps like that." The woman laughed. "I know what you mean," she said. "I get mad and write a letter and then I tear it up." The old man gave her a condescending look and said, "That so? But I don't suppose yours are of a political nature." He bent his gaze again to the choice of adhesives.

This first undertaking was duck soup for Lottie. I did not even have to exchange a word with the woman; I saw Miss Fagin lift up *that hat* and give me the high sign, and we moved away, she down one aisle and I down the other, now and again catching a glimpse of each other through the throngs. We met at the foot of the second counter, where notions were sold.

"Fun, huh?" said Lottie, and I nodded, although I felt wholly dreary. "I want some crochet hooks," she said. "Price the rickrack."

This time the clerk was adding up her receipts and did not even look at me or at a woman who was angrily and in vain trying to buy a paper of pins. Out went Lottie's scrawny hand, up went her domed chimney. In this way for some time she bagged sitting birds: a tea strainer (there was no one at all at that counter), a box of Mrs. Carpenter's All Purpose Nails, the rubber gloves I had said I wanted, and four packages of mixed seeds. Now you have some idea of the size of Lottie Jump's hat.

I was nervous, not from being her accomplice but from being in this crowd on an empty stomach, and I was getting tired—we had been in the store for at least an hour—and the whole enterprise seemed pointless. There wasn't a thing in her hat I wanted—not even the rubber gloves. But in exact proportion as my spirits descended, Lottie's rose; clearly she had only been target-practicing and now she was moving in for the kill.

We met beside the books of paper dolls, for reconnaissance. "I'm gonna get me a pair of pearl beads," said Lottie. "You go fuss with the hairpins, hear?"

Luck, combined with her skill, would have stayed with Lottie, and her hat would have been a cornucopia by the end of the afternoon if, at the very moment her hand went out for the string of beads, that idiosyncrasy of mine had not struck me full force. I had never known it to come with so few preliminaries; probably this was so because I was oppressed by all the masses of bodies poking and pushing me, and all the open mouths breathing in my face. Anyhow, right then, at the crucial time, I *had to be alone.*

I stood staring down at the bone hairpins for a moment, and when the girl behind the counter said, "What kind does Mother want, hon? What color is Mother's hair?" I looked past her and across at Lottie and I said, "Your brother isn't the only one in your family that doesn't have any brains." The clerk, astonished, turned to look where I was looking and caught Lottie in the act of lifting up her hat to put the pearls inside. She had unwisely chosen a long strand and was having a little trouble; I had the nasty thought that it looked as if her brains were leaking out.

The clerk, not able to deal with this emergency herself, frantically punched her bell and cried, "Floorwalker! Mr. Bellamy! I've caught a thief!"

Momentarily there was a violent hush—then such a clamor as you have never heard. Bells rang, babies howled, crockery crashed to the floor as people stumbled in their rush to the arena.

Mr. Bellamy, nineteen years old but broad of shoulder and jaw, was instantly standing beside Lottie, holding her arm with one hand while with the other he removed her hat to reveal to the overjoyed audience that incredible array of merchandise. Her hair all wild, her face a mask of innocent bewilderment, Lottie Jump, the scurvy thing, pretended to be deaf and dumb. She pointed at the rubber gloves and then she pointed at me, and Mr. Bellamy, able at last to prove his mettle, said "Aha!" and, still holding Lottie, moved around the counter to me and grabbed *my* arm. He gave the hat to the clerk and asked her kindly to accompany him and his red-handed catch to the manager's office.

I don't know where Lottie is now—whether she is on the stage or in jail. If her performance after our arrest meant anything, the first is quite as likely as the second. (I never saw her again, and for all I know she lit out of town that night on a freight train. Or perhaps her whole family decamped as suddenly as they had arrived; ours was a most transient population. You can be sure I made no attempt to find her again, and for months I avoided going anywhere near Arapahoe Creek or North Hill.) She never said a word but kept making signs with her fingers, ad-libbing the whole thing. They tested her hearing by shooting off a popgun right in her ear and she never batted an eyelid.

They called up my father, and he came over from the Safeway on the double. I heard very little of what he said because I was crying so hard, but one thing I did hear him say was "Well young lady, I guess you've seen to it that I'll have to part company with my good friend Judge Bay." I tried to defend myself, but it was useless. The manager, Mr. Bellamy, the clerk, and my father patted Lottie on the shoulder, and the clerk said, "Poor afflicted child." For being a poor, afflicted child, they gave her a bag of hard candy, and she gave them the most fraudulent smile of gratitude, and slobbered a little, and shuffled out, holding her empty hat in front of her like a beggar-man. I hate Lottie Jump to this day, but I have to hand it to her—she was a genius.

The floorwalker would have liked to see me sentenced to the reform school for life, I am sure, but the manager said that considering this was my first offense, he would let my father attend to my punishment.. The old-maid clerk, who looked precisely like Emmy Schmalz, clucked her tongue and shook her head at me. My father hustled me out of the office and out of the store and into the car and home, muttering the entire time; now and again I'd hear the words "morals" and "nowadays."

What's the use of telling the rest? You know what happened. Daddy on second thoughts decided not to hang his head in front of Judge Bay but to make use of his friendship in this time of need, and he took me to see the scary old curmudgeon at his house. All I remember of that long declamation, during which the Judge sat behind his desk never taking his eyes off me, was the warning "I want you to give this a great deal of thought, Miss. I want you to search and seek in the innermost corners of your conscience and root out every bit of badness." Oh, *him!* Why, listen, if I'd rooted out all the badness in me, there wouldn't have been anything left of me. My mother cried for days because she had nurtured an outlaw and was ashamed to show her face at the neighborhood store; my father was silent, and he often looked at me. Stella, who was a prig, said, "And to think you did it at *Christmas*time!" As for Jack—well, Jack a couple of times did not know how close he came to seeing glory when I had a butcher knife in my hand. It was Polecat this and Polecat that until I nearly went off my rocker. Tess, of course, didn't know what was going on, and asked so many questions that finally I told her to go to Helen Hunt Jackson in a savage tone of voice.

Good old Muff.

It is not true that you don't learn by experience. At any rate, I did that time. I began immediately to have two or three friends at a time—to be sure, because of the stigma on me, they were by no means the élite of Carlyle Hill Grade—and never again when that terrible need to be alone arose did I let fly. I would say, instead, "I've got a headache. I'll have to go home and take an aspirin," or "Gosh all hemlocks, I forgot—I've got to go to the dentist."

After the scandal died down, I got into the Campfire Girls. It was through pull, of course, since Stella had been a respected member for two years and my mother was a friend of the leader. But it turned out all right. Even Muff did not miss our periods of companionship, because about that time she grew up and started having literally millions of kittens.

Jean Stafford

☐ Emily is convinced that she is a "bad character." Why do you think she believes that? How does her behavior affect her family and friends?

☐ What influences Emily to change her behavior? Do you think that Emily also changes her opinion of herself? Explain your answer.

☐ Emily thinks that her family doesn't love her. Do you think she is justified in feeling this way? Why?

☐ Since Emily never sees Lottie after the ten-cent store incident, she never knows whether Lottie ended up on stage or in jail. What do you think happened to Lottie?

■ ■

■ The characters Lottie and Emily use expressions that are appropriate to the time in which the story is set. However, many have become outdated. List each outdated expression in the story and find a current term with a similar meaning.

■ The "friendship" of Lottie Jump and Emily Vanderpool is best observed in the following scenes: at Emily's house when they first meet; in the trolley car ride when they go downtown; and in the ten-cent store where they are caught shoplifting. Use these three scenes in a one-act play. Set up dialogue and action for each scene as found in a play script.

Lucinda Matlock

I went to the dances at Chandlerville,
And played snap-out at Winchester.
One time we changed partners,
Driving home in the moonlight of middle June,
And then I found Davis.
We were married and lived together for seventy years,
Enjoying, working, raising the twelve children,
Eight of whom we lost
Ere I had reached the age of sixty.
I spun, I wove, I kept the house, I nursed the sick,
I made the garden, and for holiday
Rambled over the fields where sang the larks,
And by Spoon River gathering many a shell,
And many a flower and medicinal weed—
Shouting to the wooded hills, singing to the green valleys.
At ninety-six I had lived enough, that is all,
And passed to a sweet repose.
What is this I hear of sorrow and weariness,
Anger, discontent, and drooping hopes?
Degenerate sons and daughters,
Life is too strong for you—
It takes life to love Life.

Edgar Lee Masters

Joyrider

"For joy rides in stupendous coverings"
Hart Crane

Call, from behind dark glasses,
Skin-tight jeans,
Joy that rides in red, streamlined
Voyage at the curb,
Door unlocked, a gift of speed
Away from boredom into necessary night.
Fit a stolen key into electric pulse.
Go, find the end. Cruise for joy,
Race, corner, idle, listen
To the engine's luring hum . . .
    For joy rides in stupendous coverings . . .

Eat a chocolate bar, smoke a cigar,
Crumple the wrapper, crush out the butt
In the ashtray of leisure.
Lower the pushbutton top to uncover
The city's glittering neon lights
Striking dark glasses with their colored lure.
Ride! Ride through joy's stupendous cover;
When the siren wails stop,
Slump in the cell, stare through bars
At the sky of fancy, mutter, "Joy, joy,
Who's the old rider wearing my face?"

James Schevill

Fifteen

South of the bridge on Seventeenth
I found back of the willows one summer
day a motorcycle with engine running
as it lay on its side, ticking over
slowly in the high grass. I was fifteen.

I admired all that pulsing gleam, the
shiny flanks, the demure headlights
fringed where it lay; I led it gently
to the road and stood with that
companion, ready and friendly. I was fifteen.

We could find the end of a road, meet
the sky on out Seventeenth. I thought about
hills, and patting the handle got back a
confident opinion. On the bridge we indulged
a forward feeling, a tremble. I was fifteen.

Thinking, back farther in the grass I found
the owner, just coming to, where he had flipped
over the rail. He had blood on his hand, was pale—
I helped him walk to his machine. He ran his hand
over it, called me good man, roared away.

I stood there, fifteen.

William Stafford

The Skaters

Graceful and sure with youth, the skaters glide
Upon the frozen pond. Unending rings
Expand upon the ice, contract, divide,
Till motion seems the shape that movement brings,

And shape is constant in the moving blade.
Ignorant of the beauty they invent,
Confirmed in their hard strength, the youths evade
Their frail suspension on an element,

This frozen pond that glisters in the cold.
Through all the warming air they turn and spin,
And do not feel that they grow old
Above the fragile ice they scrape and thin.

John Williams

John Pappas Tries Out for the Mets

John Pappas knew what he wanted—
a chance to try out for
the pitching staff of the New York Mets.
That was why he was at their
spring training camp in Florida.
And that was where he intended to
stay until he got that chance.

John Pappas appeared on the second day of spring training. He was thin and pale, and he looked about seventeen years old. He said he was twenty-one and that he had come to St. Petersburg, Florida, to be a pitcher for the New York Mets. Nobody knew what to do with him.

In any other major league clubhouse that spring, the equipment manager or the assistant trainer or maybe even the bat boy would have heaved John Pappas out the door. But this was the second day of the Mets' very first spring, and no one was sure enough of his own job to make a decision about someone else. So Pappas just stood quietly in the hushed, green-carpeted clubhouse, his sneakers under one arm, his glove under the other.

Out on the field, a collection of strangers with hopes was trying to sort itself into a team. Rabbit-quick rookies made impossible leaping catches—always when the coaches weren't looking—and the older players, some of whom had once been stars with other teams, tried to sweat themselves down into shape for the long season ahead. The borderline players worked hardest of all, running extra laps around the outfield, taking long turns in the batting cage, and chattering "Attaboy, baby, show him the hummer, good hands, chuck it in there," because Casey Stengel, manager of the Mets, had a reputation for favoring players with spirit and hustle. The borderline players knew if they didn't make it with this brand-new team they would probably slide right on out of the major leagues.

Pappas stood for a long time in the clubhouse, politely but firmly telling anyone who asked that he had no intention of budging until someone from the Mets gave him a tryout. Finally, a tall sad-faced man came out of a side office and looked into Pappas's steady brown eyes. He introduced himself as John Murphy, an official of the new club.

"Where are you from?" asked Murphy.

"New York City," said Pappas.

"When was the last time you threw a ball?"

"Last Sunday, in New York," said Pappas.

Murphy's eyes narrowed, and he smiled, a triumphant little smile. "It snowed in New York last Sunday."

Pappas nodded. "Yes, sir. But not underneath the Triborough Bridge."

Murphy's eyes widened. He motioned Pappas to a wooden bench in front of the lockers and sat down beside him. The young man said he had bought four regulation National League baseballs and pitched them at a painted square on a concrete wall under the bridge. After he was satisfied, he ran for several miles in a nearby park. Then he packed for spring training.

He had arrived in St. Petersburg at three o'clock that morning, he said, after his first airplane trip. It was also the first time he had ever been more than a hundred miles from his parents' home in Astoria, Queens.

Murphy listened and nodded and pulled at his long, sad face. Then he stood up. "We're not holding tryouts here, John." He pointed through the open clubhouse door to the practice ball fields. "There would be a million guys out there if we were."

"I don't see a million guys out there," said Pappas seriously and softly. When Murphy shot him a hard glance to see if he was being smart, Pappas looked down at his black pointy shoes.

Murphy sighed. "You play high-school ball?"

"My high school didn't have a team, Mr. Murphy, but I

played Police Athletic League ball. I don't remember which precinct."

"Did anyone ever say you were professional material?"

"No, sir."

"Do your parents know you came down here for a tryout?"

"No one knows, Mr. Murphy."

Murphy sat down again, and his voice became gentle. "Do you go to school?"

"I was going to City College at night, but I stopped going to classes. And I quit my job. I was working in a furniture store. I told my mother I was coming down for a week's vacation and then I'd look for another job."

Almost wearily, Murphy said, "This is not a tryout camp."

Pappas took a deep breath. "Mr. Murphy, I don't have much experience, and I'm willing to spend a few years in the minors. But I think I can pitch, and I want to find out now. I want to succeed in the world, and I can do it if I set my mind to it."

"Of course you can," said Murphy, "but there are many ways to succeed in the world besides major league baseball."

"I'm going to stay here until someone looks at me pitch," said Pappas, running a bony hand through his black pompadour. "If they tell me I'm no good, I'll just finish my vacation and go home and set my mind to something else."

Murphy stared at Pappas for a long time. "Okay, John," he said. "You get yourself a catcher and a place to throw and call me up and I'll come over and look at you."

They shook hands, and Pappas, smiling now, bounded out of the clubhouse. "Thanks, thanks a lot," he called back over his shoulder. "I'll see you soon."

Murphy watched him go, then shook his head at us and walked back into his office. Another newspaperman turned to me and said, "That's a flaky kid for you. I don't know why Murphy wastes his time."

"What do you mean flaky?" I said. "He might really have it; he might be a star. And who says Murphy could tell from one tryout?"

"Johnny Murphy was once a great relief pitcher for the

Yankees," said the other newspaperman, "and I think you're a flaky kid, too."

The weather was erratic in St. Petersburg that week, sometimes cool, almost always windy. John Pappas ran in the mornings near his motel and found youngsters to catch his pitching. Three days after he first showed up, a local newspaper arranged for Pappas to use a nearby high-school ball field, and Murphy promised to drive out to watch him pitch. Murphy said he would even bring a professional catcher.

The morning of his tryout Pappas returned to the Mets spring-training camp at Miller Huggins Field and found a seat in the sun on the grandstand. A little less pale now, but still thin and tense, he sat in a crowd of elderly tourists and pensioners and watched the Mets work out. I sat with him for a little while. He pointed at four young Met pitchers who were taking turns throwing for batting practice.

"That could be me," he said.

At 3:38 P.M. on February 23, 1962, John Pappas had his chance. While a dozen newspapermen and photographers watched, he strode onto a scruffy pitching mound and put everything in his slight body behind the baseballs he threw at Bill Whalen, a young catcher from the Mets' camp. Pappas threw for eighteen minutes in silence. He was wild, and he wasn't very fast.

At precisely 3:56 P.M., Murphy walked out to the mound and put his arm around Pappas's thin shoulders. "All you have is guts, son," he said.

They shook hands. Murphy thanked Pappas for giving the Mets a chance to look him over. Very kindly, he told Pappas to forget about professional baseball. Maybe if he were only fifteen years old it might make sense to keep at it, but at twenty-one he had too far to go and too much to learn.

Pappas thanked Murphy for giving him a tryout. He said he was satisfied and now he was going back to New York.

"I always would have wondered," said Pappas, "but now I know. I just wasn't good enough. Now I'll look for something else, some other way of being somebody."

The ball field slowly emptied, and soon there was just Pappas, and two or three of the younger newspapermen who had secretly hoped that this thin, sallow, round-shouldered young clerk would turn out to have an arm like a bullwhip, a live fast-ball that hummed, and a curve that danced in the sun. I think we were more disappointed than he was, and we were talking mostly for ourselves on the ride back to town, telling Pappas that there were other ways to succeed in the world besides major league baseball and that he was way ahead of the game; after all, how many men actually got a chance to try out, to find out once and for all? Pappas nodded and agreed and smiled and thanked us for our encouragement.

It was dusk when we reached his motel. The last time I saw John Pappas he was framed in the car window, and he said: "You know, I'm sorry they didn't give me a chance to hit. I'm not a bad hitter. And I play the outfield too."

Robert Lipsyte

☐ The conversations between John Pappas and John Murphy reveal a great deal about them. What kind of men do they seem to be? What attitude does the author seem to have toward them? How do you know?

☐ Early in this selection, John Pappas vows that he will give up baseball if he fails the tryout. What does he say at the end of the selection that indicates he might not keep his vow? What do these two statements reveal about his sense of personal direction?

■ ■

■ If you were a photographer for a newspaper assigned to cover the Mets spring training camp, what scenes would you photograph in this story? For each photograph write a one-line description that could be used as a caption.

How to Win at Basketball: Cheat

Why did Bill Cosby, the famous humorist,
have to learn karate
in order to play basketball?

When I played basketball in the slums of Philadelphia—outdoors on concrete courts—there was never a referee. You had to call your own fouls. So the biggest argument was always about whether you called the foul *before* the shot went in, or whether you had waited to see if the ball went in. See, if you yelled "foul," you didn't get the basket. You just got the ball out-of-bounds.

Sometimes you called a *light* foul. Like you have a guy driving in on you and you punch him in the eye a little. That's a light foul in the playgrounds.

Another light foul is submarining a guy who's driving in on you. He comes down on the concrete, and you visit him every two weeks in the hospital. Of course, there is always a pole sitting in the middle of the court. Something has to hold up the basket. So you let a guy drive in, and you just kind of screen him a little bit, right into the pole. This is where you visit him three times a week in the hospital.

There's always a big argument, too, about whether you stepped out-of-bounds or not. That's a four-hour argument. So usually you take one shot—20-minute argument. Another shot —20-minute argument. Out-of-bounds—four-hour argument.

So this one game—the winner is the first team to score 20 points—can go maybe two weeks. The most important thing is to remember the score from day to day. Sometimes you argue four hours about *that*.

To play on any team outdoors, you have to have a pair of old jeans that you cut off and shred a little bit above the knees so they look like beachcomber pants. You get an old sweat shirt of some university—mine was Temple—and you go outside to the playground, and play basketball all day, until dark, and your mother has to come get you.

Let me say something about mothers. When I was a kid, mothers were never really interested in sports. Even if you became a fantastic star, your mother was probably the last person to know. She was more concerned with you being on time for dinner.

My mother was a fantastic color changer. Whatever color my uniform was, my mother would always put it into the washing machine with different-colored stuff—the red bedspread, the green curtains, the yellow tablecloth, or the purple bathroom rug. And when the uniform came out, instead of being white, it would be avocado.

I've worn a pink uniform, and I've worn a running yellow-and-blue uniform—which of course startled my teammates quite a bit. One time, I had to learn how to use karate in order to answer for a pale-lavender uniform.

Later, I graduated from playground basketball to indoor basketball. I played for a place called the Wissahickon Boys' Club along with a very famous defensive back by the name of Herb Adderley.

Well, very few teams could whip the Wissahickon Boys' Club on our own court, mainly because our court was different. First of all, the floor hadn't been varnished and the out-of-bounds lines hadn't been painted since the day the gym was built, about two weeks after Dr. Naismith invented basketball. We didn't have to see them. We could feel where they were. Our sneakers had soles as thick as a piece of paper. But it was rough on the other team.

So was the ball. We used a leather ball that had been played with outside—in the dark of night, in the rain, in the snow. It was about as heavy as a medicine ball, and just as lively. There were stones and pieces of glass stuck into it, and it never had enough air, because the valve leaked. You could wear yourself out just trying to dribble it.

Now about the basket. The rim was loose, and hanging, and shaking. And all you had to do was kind of lay that heavy ball up softly. The rim acted like a trampoline. It lifted the ball up and threw it through the center of the hoop and you always had two points.

Another thing about playing at the Wissahickon Boys' Club. We would get ol' Weird Harold, who was six feet nine and weighed about 90 pounds, to mark black X's all over the backboard. Now, only our team knew what each X stood for. See, we aimed maybe two inches under a mark, and, zap, two points. If you followed our mark, you'd miss the rim. We always had something going for ourselves.

The ceiling in the gym was only 15 feet high. For those who may not know that much about basketball, that means our ceiling was only five feet above the rim of the basket itself. When other teams came to play us, they weren't aware right away that the ceiling was low. So when they shot the ball, they hit the ceiling—which was out-of-bounds. And we would get the ball. Meanwhile, we had practiced shooting our jump shots and set shots on a direct line drive. No arch, no nothing—just straight ahead into the basket. Sort of Woody Sauldsberry style.

We also had a hot-water pipe that ran around the wall, and the wall of the gym was out-of-bounds. If you touched the wall or anything, you were out-of-bounds. So whenever a guy on the other team would go up for a rebound or a jump shot, or drive into the basket, we would kind of screen him into the hot-water pipe.

At the Wissahickon Boys' Club, we had graduated to the point where we had referees for the games. We had them because they were honest and fair and impartial. Which is what they teach at boys clubs. Also because we were playing teams from other neighborhoods and had to finish the games in one day. The referees cut down on the long arguments.

We had two steady refs whom we named Mr. Magoo and

The Bat. You might say they did not have Superman vision. They more or less had to make their calls on what they could hear. Like if they heard a slap, and thought they saw the ball fly out of a guy's hands, they cried "foul" for hacking. So whenever a guy would go up for a rebound or something, all we had to do was just give him a little nudge, and boom! He'd wind up against the wall and probably that hot-water pipe. His screams would tell The Bat and Mr. Magoo he was out-of-bounds.

When new teams came down to play us and saw our uniforms, which consisted of heavy old long-sleeved flannel pajama tops over below-the-knee corduroy knickers, they'd call us "turkeys" and all kinds of chicken names. Maybe we weren't cool. But we were protected from that hot-water pipe.

One time, Cryin' Charlie's mother had his PJ tops in the washing machine at game time, and we had to make him non-playing coach that day so he wouldn't cry.

In the middle of the court, we had five boards that happened to be about the loosest boards that you ever stepped on in your life. So that while dribbling downcourt on a fast break, if you hit one of those five boards, the ball would not come back to you. Many times, a guy on the other team would dribble downcourt on the fast break, and all of a sudden he'd be running, and his arm would be pumping, but there was no ball coming back up to him. All we had to do was just stand around at the loose boards, and without even stickin' the guy, let him go ahead and do his Lamont Cranston dribble, and we could pick up the ball, dead and waiting, right there. Whenever *we* went on a fast break, we dribbled *around* those loose boards.

One team I remember we lost to was the Nicetown Club for Boys & Girls. We played in their gym. They had a balcony that extended out over one side of the court about ten feet. It was almost exactly the same height as the rim of the basket. So if you went up for a jumper, the balcony would block your shot. The defense of the Nicetown Club was to force the flow of your offense to the side of the court with the balcony. When we tried to shoot from there, the Bill Russell balcony would block the shot, and the ball would bounce back and hit our man in the eye. Whenever *they* came downcourt, they would play on the free side of the floor away from the balcony.

I would say, on a home-and-home basis, the Wissahickon Boys' Club and the Nicetown Club were even.

In high school, I had one of the greatest jump shots—from two feet out—anybody ever saw. The only man who stopped me was Wilt Chamberlain.

We played Wilt's high school, Overbrook, and they had a guy on the team by the name of Ira Davis, who was a great track man. He ran the 100 in like nine-point-something, and a few years later was in the Olympic Games. Ira was great on the fast break. So Chamberlain would stand under our basket and growl at us. And when he growled, guys would just throw the ball at him—to try and hit him with it. And he would catch it and throw it downcourt to Ira Davis, who would score 200 points on the fast break. We lost to them something like 800 to 14.

My best shot was where I would dribble in quickly, stop, fake the man playing me into the air, and then go up for my two-foot jump shot. Well, I was very surprised when I found Mr. Chamberlain waiting under the basket for me. I faked, and faked and faked and faked and faked, and then I threw the ball at him and tried to hit him. But he caught it and threw it downcourt to Ira Davis: 802 to 14.

So then we tried to razzle-dazzle him. But for some reason, he could always follow the ball with that one eye of his in the middle of his forehead. And of course, the only thing we could do was just throw the ball at him.

We had one play we used on Wilt that had some success. We had one kid that was completely crazy. He wasn't afraid of anything in the world. Not even the Big Dipper. He was about as big as Mickey Rooney, and we had him run out on the court and punch Chamberlain right in the kneecap. And when Chamberlain bent over to grab our guy, we shot our jumpers. That foul alone was worth our 14 points.

Now that I'm a celebrity making a million dollars a year, we have Celebrity Basketball. I play with guys like James Garner, Jim Brown, Don Adams, Sidney Poitier, Mike Connors, Mickey Rooney, and Jack Lemmon.

In Celebrity Basketball, you pull up to the fabulous Forum in your Rolls-Royce, and your chauffeur puts you in a beach chair and wheels you out on the court. And after each shot, you have a catered affair.

And the ball. The pros wish they could find a ball this great. It's gold covered and has a little transistor motor inside, with radar and a homing device, and it dribbles and shoots itself.

A 60-piece orchestra plays background music while you're down on the court, and starlet cheerleaders are jumping up and down. After every basket, we all stop and give the guy who scored it a standing ovation.

Another thing about when I used to play basketball in the playgrounds. If you went to a strange playground, you didn't introduce yourself. You had to prove yourself first. No names.

"Over here, my man."

"Yeah, nice play, my man."

Later on, if you earned it, you'd be given a name: Gunner, My Man or Herman or Shorty or something.

Now, when we play the Celebrity games, they come out on the court and they say, "Hi, my name is such and such. I'm from so forth and so on," and the whole thing. And I say, "Oh, very nice to meet you."

But later, during the game, I forget the cat's name anyway and I just go right back to "Over here, my man. I'm free in the corner, my man." And I'm back in the old neighborhood.

Bill Cosby

☐ Bill Cosby uses humorous exaggeration to describe the way he and his friends played basketball in Philadelphia. Which incidents are described in exaggerated language?

☐ Humor is also achieved through Cosby's use of understatement, as in his description of the "light" foul. Find other examples of understatement. Why is this an effective means of achieving humor?

☐ Behind the surface humor of this article, Bill Cosby reveals some serious problems that he and his friends had to deal with. What are some and how did they deal with them?

■ ■

■ Choose a favorite sport and make up a set of rules and conditions that would guarantee that your team would win. Describe the equipment, playing area, and uniforms in the exaggerated manner used by Bill Cosby. Try to make the rules of this sport as humorous as you can. Remember, your team must win!

■ Bill Cosby describes many of the players and basketball techniques of the Wissahickon Basketball Team. Prepare an official handbook of the basketball team. List the players and any additional names needed to complete the squad. Beside each player's name list the basketball technique for which he is famous. Provide a history of wins and losses and an official scorecard. You may wish to include an illustration of the home court and a drawing of the official uniform of the team.

■ As a member of the Wissahickon Basketball Team, write a letter of appreciation to the referees thanking them for their assistance during the season. Adopt a genuinely serious tone or take on a mock serious tone to tease the referee group.

Training
for the Wildlife

To the North American Indians,
superb physiques and wisdom were
considered important qualities of manhood.
Each quality was developed through
vigorous training. In this selection
Charles Eastman (Hakadah), born to the
wild life as a member of a Sioux tribe,
recalls his boyhood education in the 1880's.

It seems to be a popular idea that all the characteristic skill of the Indian is instinctive and hereditary. This is a mistake. All the stoicism and patience of the Indian are acquired traits, and continual practice alone makes him master of the art of woodcraft. Physical training and dieting were not neglected. I remember that I was not allowed to have beef soup or warm drink. The soup was for the old men. General rules for the young were never to take their food very hot, nor to drink much water.

My uncle, who educated me up to the age of fifteen years, was a strict disciplinarian and a good teacher. When I left the teepee in the morning, he would say: "Hakadah, look closely to everything you see"; and at evening, on my return, he used often to catechize me for an hour.

"On which side of the trees is the lighter-colored bark? On which side do they have most regular branches?"

It was his custom to let me name all the new birds that I had seen during the day. I would name them according to the color or the shape of the bill or their song or the appearance and locality of the nest—in fact, anything about the bird that impressed me as characteristic. I made many ridiculous errors,

From *Indian Boyhood* by Charles A. Eastman. Dover Publications, Inc., New York, New York. Reprinted through permission of the publisher.

65

I must admit. He then usually informed me of the correct name. Occasionally I made a hit and this he would warmly commend.

He went much deeper into this science when I was a little older, that is, about the age of eight or nine years. He would say, for instance:

"How do you know that there are fish in yonder lake?"

"Because they jump out of the water for flies at mid-day."

He would smile at my prompt but superficial reply.

"What do you think of the little pebbles grouped together under the shallow water? and what made the pretty curved marks in the sandy bottom and the little sandbanks? Where do you find the fish-eating birds? Have the inlet and the outlet of a lake anything to do with the question?"

He did not expect a correct reply at once to all the voluminous questions that he put to me on these occasions, but he meant to make me observant and a good student of nature.

"Hakadah," he would say to me, "you ought to follow the example of the shunktokecha (wolf). Even when he is surprised and runs for his life, he will pause to take one more look at you before he enters his final retreat. So you must take a second look at everything you see.

"It is better to view animals unobserved. I have been a witness to their courtships and their quarrels and have learned many of their secrets in this way. I was once the unseen spectator of a thrilling battle between a pair of grizzly bears and three buffaloes—a rash act for the bears, for it was in the moon of strawberries, when the buffaloes sharpen and polish their horns for bloody contests among themselves.

"I advise you, my boy, never to approach a grizzly's den from the front, but to steal up behind and throw your blanket or a stone in front of the hole. He does not usually rush for it, but first puts his head out and listens and then comes out very indifferently and sits on his haunches on the mound in front of the hole before he makes any attack. While he is exposing himself in this fashion, aim at his heart. Always be as cool as the animal himself." Thus he armed me against the cunning of savage beasts by teaching me how to outwit them.

"In hunting," he would resume, "you will be guided by the

habits of the animal you seek. Remember that a moose stays in swampy or low land or between high mountains near a spring or lake, for thirty to sixty days at a time. Most large game moves about continually, except the doe in the spring; it is then a very easy matter to find her with the fawn. Conceal yourself in a convenient place as soon as you observe any signs of the presence of either, and then call with your birchen doe-caller.

"Whichever one hears you first will soon appear in your neighborhood. But you must be very watchful, or you may be made a fawn of by a large wildcat. They understand the characteristic call of the doe perfectly well.

"When you have any difficulty with a bear or a wildcat— that is, if the creature shows signs of attacking you—you must make him fully understand that you have seen him and are aware of his intentions. If you are not well equipped for a pitched battle, the only way to make him retreat is to take a long sharp-pointed pole for a spear and rush toward him. No wild beast will face this unless he is cornered and already wounded. These fierce beasts are generally afraid of the common weapon of the larger animals—the horns, and if these are very long and sharp, they dare not risk an open fight.

"There is one exception to this rule—the grey wolf will attack fiercely when very hungry. But their courage depends upon their numbers; in this they are like white men. One wolf or two will never attack a man. They will stampede a herd of buffaloes in order to get at the calves; they will rush upon a herd of antelopes, for these are helpless; but they are always careful about attacking man."

Of this nature were the instructions of my uncle, who was widely known at that time as among the greatest of hunters of his tribe.

All boys were expected to endure hardship without complaint. In savage warfare, a young man must, of course, be an athlete and used to undergoing all sorts of privations. He must be able to go without food and water for two or three days without displaying any weakness, or to run for a day and a night without any rest. He must be able to traverse a pathless and wild country without losing his way either in the day or nighttime. He cannot refuse to do any of these things if he aspires to be a warrior.

Sometimes my uncle would waken me very early in the morning and challenge me to fast with him all day. I had to accept the challenge. We blackened our faces with charcoal, so that every boy in the village would know that I was fasting for the day. Then the little tempers would make my life a misery until the merciful sun hid behind the western hills.

I can scarcely recall the time when my stern teacher began to give sudden war whoops over my head in the morning while I was sound asleep. He expected me to leap up with perfect presence of mind, always ready to grasp a weapon of some sort and to give a shrill whoop in reply. If I was sleepy or startled and hardly knew what I was about, he would ridicule me and say that I need never expect to sell my scalp dear. Often he would vary these tactics by shooting off his gun just outside of the lodge while I was yet asleep, at the same time giving blood-curdling yells. After a time I became used to this.

When Indians went upon the warpath, it was their custom to try the new warriors thoroughly before coming to an engagement. For instance, when they were near a hostile camp, they would select the novices to go after the water and make them do all sorts of things to prove their courage. In accordance with this idea, my uncle used to send me after water when we camped after dark in a strange place. Perhaps the country was full of wild beasts, and, for all I knew, there might be scouts from hostile bands of Indians lurking in that very neighborhood.

Yet I never objected, for that would show cowardice. I picked my way through the woods, dipped my pail in the water, and hurried back, always careful to make as little noise as a cat. Because I was only a boy, my heart would leap at every crackling of a dry twig or distant hooting of an owl, until, at last, I reached our teepee. Then my uncle would perhaps say: "Ah, Hakadah, you are a thorough warrior," empty out the precious contents of the pail, and order me to go a second time.

Imagine how I felt! But I wished to be a brave man as much as a white boy desires to be a great lawyer or even President of the United States. Silently I would take the pail and endeavor to retrace my footsteps in the dark.

With all this, our manners and morals were not neglected. I was made to respect the adults and especially the aged. I was not allowed to join in their discussions, nor even to speak in their presence, unless requested to do so. Indian etiquette was very strict, and among the requirements was that of avoiding the direct address. A term of relationship or some title of courtesy was commonly used instead of the personal name by those who wished to show respect. We were taught generosity to the poor and reverence for the "Great Mystery." Religion was the basis of all Indian training.

I recall to the present day some of the kind warnings and reproofs that my good grandmother was wont to give me. "Be strong of heart—be patient!" she used to say. She told me of a young chief who was noted for his uncontrollable temper. While in one of his rages he attempted to kill a woman, for which he was slain by his own band and left unburied as a mark of disgrace—his body was simply covered with green grass. If I ever lost my temper, she would say:

"Hakadah, control yourself, or you will be like that young man I told you of, and lie under a *green blanket!*"

In the old days, no young man was allowed to use tobacco in any form until he had become an acknowledged warrior and had achieved a record. If a youth should seek a wife before he had reached the age of twenty-two or twenty-three, and been recognized as a brave man, he was sneered at and considered an ill-bred Indian. He must also be a skillful hunter. An Indian cannot be a good husband unless he brings home plenty of game.

These precepts were in the line of our training for the wild life.

Charles A. Eastman
(*Ohiyesa*)

☐ How did Hakadah's uncle turn him into an observant student of nature? Why was this training important to Hakadah?

☐ Compare the differences in training received by the Sioux Indian youths and the training received by young people in our country today.

☐ Hakadah is educated by a loving but stern uncle. Why doesn't Hakadah rebel against his uncle's discipline? What conditions of Indian life described in this selection demand obedience of the Indian youth?

☐ Are there any parts of Hakadah's "training for the wild life" that would be valuable for young people today? Discuss.

■ ■

■ Try an experiment that Hakadah's uncle might have assigned to you. Choose any familiar object and think of its color, shape, texture, and unique features. Write a description or draw the familiar object as carefully as you can. Compare your description or drawing with the actual object. What did you see and what did you miss? Did you follow the Uncle's advice and "look closely to everything"?

■ Do a memory experiment. Try to recapture what you saw, heard, and felt during the first five minutes of this class. Record your impressions in a series of words and phrases. Check your recollection with other people.

■ Consider some of your own personal characteristics. Is your style of dress, your speech habits, manner of walking, and general behavior similar to those of people you know? Do you imitate any of the characteristics of parents, other relatives, friends, or acquaintances?

Gee, You're So Beautiful
that It's Starting to Rain

Oh, Marcia,
I want your long blonde beauty
to be taught in high school,
so kids will learn that God
lives like music in the skin
and sounds like a sunshine harpsichord.
I want high school report cards
   to look like this:

Playing with Gentle Glass Things
   A

Computer Magic
   A

Writing Letters to Those You Love
   A

Finding out about Fish
   A

Marcia's Long Blonde Beauty
   A + !

Richard Brautigan

In the Barrio

*This barrio[1] was not like the one he had
left in Mazatlán, Mexico. Ernesto found
himself entering a strange, new world in
the barrio of Sacramento, California.*

We found the Americans as strange in their
customs as they probably found us. Immediately we discovered
that there were no *mercados* [2] and that when shopping you did
not put the groceries in a *chiquihuite*[3]. Instead everything was
in cans or in cardboard boxes or each item was put in a brown
paper bag. There were neighborhood grocery stores at the corners and some big ones uptown, but no *mercado*. The grocers
did not give children a *pilón*[4], they did not stand at the door and
coax you to come in and buy, as they did in Mazatlán. The
fruits and vegetables were displayed on counters instead of
being piled up on the floor. The stores smelled of fly spray and
oiled floors, not of fresh pineapple and limes.

Neither was there a plaza, only parks which had no band-
stands, no concerts every Thursday, no Judases exploding on
Holy Week, and no promenades of boys going one way and girls
the other. There were no parks in the *barrio;* and the ones up-

---

[1] *barrio* (bä′ryo)   [2] *mercados* (mer kä′ᵀHōs)
[3] *chiquihuite* (chē kē hwē′tē)   [4] *pilón* (pē lōn′)

town were cold and rainy in winter, and in summer there was no place to sit except on the grass. When there were celebrations nobody set off rockets in the parks, much less on the street in front of your house to announce to the neighborhood that a wedding or a baptism was taking place. Sacramento did not have a *mercado* and a plaza with the cathedral to one side and the Palacio de Gobierno on another to make it obvious that there and nowhere else was the center of the town.

It was just as puzzling that the Americans did not live in *vecindades*[5], like our block on Leandro Valle. Even in the alleys, where people knew one another better, the houses were fenced apart, without central courts to wash clothes, talk, and play with the other children. Like the city, the Sacramento *barrio* did not have a place which was the middle of things for everyone.

In more personal ways we had to get used to the Americans. They did not listen if you did not speak loudly, as they always did. In the Mexican style, people would know that you were enjoying their jokes tremendously if you merely smiled and shook a little, as if you were trying to swallow your mirth. In the American style there was little difference between a laugh and a roar, and until you got used to them you could hardly tell whether the boisterous Americans were roaring mad or roaring happy.

It was Doña Henriqueta more than Gustavo or José who talked of these oddities and classified them as agreeable or deplorable. It was she also who pointed out the pleasant surprises of the American way. When a box of rolled oats with a picture of red carnations on the side was emptied, there was a plate or a bowl or a cup with blue designs. We ate the strange stuff regularly for breakfast and we soon had a set of the beautiful dishes. Rice and beans we bought in cotton bags of colored prints. The bags were unsewed, washed, ironed, and made into gaily designed towels, napkins, and handkerchiefs. The American stores also gave small green stamps which were pasted in a book to exchange for prizes. We didn't have to run to the corner with the garbage; a collector came for it.

With remarkable fairness and never-ending wonder we kept adding to our list the pleasant and the repulsive in the ways of the Americans. It was my second acculturation.

---

[5] *vecindades* (ve sēn dä′ᵀHās)

74

The older people of the *barrio*, except in those things which they had to do like the Americans because they had no choice, remained Mexican. Their language at home was Spanish. They were continuously taking up collections to pay somebody's funeral expenses or to help someone who had had a serious accident. Cards were sent to you to attend a burial where you would throw a handful of dirt on top of the coffin and listen to tearful speeches at the graveside. At every baptism a new *compadre*[6] and a new *comadre*[7] joined the family circle. New Year greeting cards were exchanged, showing angels and cherubs in bright colors sprinkled with grains of mica so that they glistened like gold dust. At the family parties the huge pot of steaming tamales was still the center of attention, the *atole*[8] served on the side with chunks of brown sugar for sucking and crunching. If the party lasted long enough, someone produced a guitar, the men took over and the singing or *corridos*[9] began.

In the *barrio* there were no individuals who had official titles or who were otherwise recognized by everybody as important people. The reason must have been that there was no place in the public business of the city of Sacramento for the Mexican immigrants. We only rented a corner of the city and as long as we paid the rent on time everything else was decided at City Hall or the County Court House, where Mexicans went only when they were in trouble. Nobody from the *barrio* ever ran for mayor or city councilman. For us the most important public officials were the policemen who walked their beats, stopped fights, and hauled drunks to jail in a paddy wagon we called *La Julia.*

The one institution we had that gave the *colonia*[10] some kind of image was the *Comisión Honorífica*, a committee picked by the Mexican Consul in San Francisco to organize the celebration of the *Cinco de Mayo* and the Sixteenth of September, the anniversaries of the battle of Puebla and the beginning of our War of Independence. These were the two events which stirred everyone in the *barrio*, for what we were celebrating was not only the heroes of Mexico but also the feeling that we were still Mexicans ourselves. On these occasions there was a dance preceded by speeches and a concert. For both the *cinco* and the sixteenth queens were elected to preside over the ceremonies.

---

[6] *compadre* (kōm pä′drä)   [7] *comadre* (kō mä′drä)   [8] *atole* (ä tō′lä)
[9] *corridos* (kō rē′ℲHōs)   [10] *colonia* (kō lō′nyä)

Between celebrations neither the politicians uptown nor the *Comisión Honorífica* attended to the daily needs of the *barrio*. This was done by volunteers—the ones who knew enough English to interpret in court, on a visit to the doctor, a call at the county hospital, and who could help make out a postal money order. By the time I had finished the third grade at the Lincoln School I was one of these volunteers. My services were not professional but they were free, except for the IOU's I accumulated from families who always thanked me with "God will pay you for it."

My clients were not *pochos* [11], Mexicans who had grown up in California, probably had even been born in the United States. They had learned to speak English of sorts and could still speak Spanish, also of sorts. They knew much more about the Americans than we did, and much less about us. The *chicanos* [12] and the *pochos* had certain feelings about one another. Concerning the *pochos*, the *chicanos* suspected that they considered themselves too good for the *barrio* but were not, for some reason, good enough for the Americans. Toward the *chicanos*, the *pochos* acted superior, amused at our confusions but not especially interested in explaining them to us. In our family when I forgot my manners, my mother would ask me if I was turning *pochito* [13].

Turning *pocho* was a half-step toward turning American. And America was all around us, in and out of the *barrio*. Abruptly we had to forget the ways of shopping in a *mercado* and learn those of shopping in a corner grocery or in a department store. The Americans paid no attention to the Sixteenth of September, but they made a great commotion about the Fourth of July. In Mazatlán Don Salvador had told us, saluting and marching as he talked to our class, that the *Cinco de Mayo* was the most glorious date in human history. The Americans had not even heard about it.

In Tucson, when I had asked my mother again if the Americans were having a revolution, the answer was: "No, but they have good schools, and you are going to one of them." We were by now settled at 418 L Street and the time had come for me to exchange a revolution for an American education.

The two of us walked south on Fifth Street one morning to the corner of Q Street and turned right. Half of the block was

---

[11] *pochos* (pō′chōs)   [12] *chicanos* (chē cä′nōs)
[13] *pochito* (pō chē′tō)

occupied by the Lincoln School. It was a three-story wooden building, with two wings that gave it the shape of a double-T connected by a central hall. It was a new building, painted yellow, with a shingled roof that was not like the red tile of the school in Mazatlán. I noticed other differences, none of them very reassuring.

We walked up the wide staircase hand in hand and through the door, which closed by itself. A mechanical contraption screwed to the top shut it behind us quietly.

Up to this point the adventure of enrolling me in the school had been carefully rehearsed. Mrs. Dodson had told us how to find it and we had circled it several times in our walks. Friends in the *barrio* explained that the director was called a principal, and that it was a lady and not a man. They assured us that there was always a person at the school who could speak Spanish.

Exactly as we had been told, there was a sign on the door in both Spanish and English: "Principal." We crossed the hall and entered the office of Miss Nettie Hopley.

Miss Hopley was at a roll-top desk to one side, sitting in a swivel chair that moved on wheels. There was a sofa against the opposite wall, flanked by two windows and a door that opened on a small balcony. Chairs were set around a table and on the walls hung framed pictures of a man with long white hair and another with a sad face and a black beard.

The principal half turned in the swivel chair to look at us over the pinch glasses crossed on the ridge of her nose. To do this she had to duck her head slightly as if she were about to step through a low doorway.

What Miss Hopley said to us we did not know but we saw in her eyes a warm welcome and when she took off her glasses and straightened up she smiled wholeheartedly, like Mrs. Dodson. We were, of course, saying nothing, only catching the friendliness of her voice and the sparkle in her eyes while she said words we did not understand. She signaled us to the table. Almost tiptoeing across the office, I maneuvered myself to keep my mother between me and the gringo lady. In a matter of seconds I had to decide whether she was a possible friend or a menace. We sat down.

Then Miss Hopley did a formidable thing. She stood up. Had she been standing when we entered she would have seemed tall. But rising from her chair she soared. And what she carried up and up with her was a buxom superstructure, firm shoulders, a straight sharp nose, full cheeks slightly molded by a curved line along the nostrils, thin lips that moved like steel springs, and a high forehead topped by hair gathered in a bun. Miss Hopley was not a giant in body but when she mobilized it to a standing position she seemed a match for giants. I decided I liked her.

She strode to a door in the far corner of the office, opened it, and called a name. A boy of about ten years appeared in the doorway. He sat down at one end of the table. He was brown like us, a plump kid with shiny black hair combed straight back, neat, cool, and faintly obnoxious.

Miss Hopley joined us with a large book and some papers in her hand. She, too, sat down and the questions and answers began by way of our interpreter. My name was Ernesto. My mother's name was Henriqueta. My birth certificate was in San Blas. Here was my last report card from the Escuela Municipal Numero 3 para Varones of Mazatlán, and so forth. Miss Hopley put things down in the book and my mother signed a card.

As long as the questions continued, Doña Henriqueta could stay and I was secure. Now that they were over, Miss Hopley saw her to the door, dismissed our interpreter, and without further ado took me by the hand and strode down the hall to Miss Ryan's first grade.

Miss Ryan took me to a seat at the front of the room, into which I shrank—the better to survey her. She was, to skinny, somewhat runty me, of a withering height when she patrolled the class. And when I least expected it, there she was, crouching by my desk, her blond radiant face level with mine, her voice patiently maneuvering me over the awful idiocies of the English language.

During the next few weeks Miss Ryan overcame my fears of tall, energetic teachers as she bent over my desk to help me with a word in the pre-primer. Step by step, she loosened me and my classmates from the safe anchorage of the desks for recitations at the blackboard and consultations at her desk.

Frequently she burst into happy announcements to the whole class. "Ito can read a sentence," and small Japanese Ito, squint-eyed and shy, slowly read aloud while the class listened in wonder: "Come, Skipper, come. Come and run." The Korean, Portuguese, Italian, and Polish first graders had similar moments of glory, no less shining than mine the day I conquered "butterfly," which I had been persistently pronouncing in standard Spanish as boo-ter-flee. "Children," Miss Ryan called for attention. "Ernesto has learned how to pronounce *butterfly!*" And I proved it with a perfect imitation of Miss Ryan. From that celebrated success, I was soon able to match Ito's progress as a sentence reader with "Come, butterfly, come fly with me."

Like Ito and several other first graders who did not know English, I received private lessons from Miss Ryan in the closet, a narrow hall off the classroom with a door at each end. Next to one of these doors Miss Ryan placed a large chair for herself and a small one for me. Keeping an eye on the class through the open door she read with me about sheep in the meadow and a frightened chicken going to see the king, coaching me out of my phonetic ruts in words like *pasture, bow-wow-wow, hay,* and *pretty,* which to my Mexican ear and eye had so many unnecessary sounds and letters. She made me watch her lips and then close my eyes as she repeated words I found hard to read. When we came to know each other better, I tried interrupting to tell Miss Ryan how we said it in Spanish. It didn't work. She only said "oh" and went on with *pasture, bow-wow-wow,* and *pretty.* It was as if in that closet we were both discovering together the secrets of the English language and grieving together over the tragedies of Bo-Peep. The main reason I was graduated with honors from the first grade was that I had fallen in love with Miss Ryan. Her radiant, no-nonsense character made us either afraid not to love her or love her so we would not be afraid, I am not sure which. It was not only that we sensed she was with it, but also that she was with us.

Like the first grade, the rest of the Lincoln School was a sampling of the lower part of town where many races made their home. My pals in the second grade were Kazushi, whose parents spoke only Japanese; Matti, a skinny Italian boy; and Manuel, a fat Portuguese who would never get into a fight but wrestled you to the ground and just sat on you. Our assortment of nationalities included Koreans, Yugoslavs, Poles, Irish, and home-grown Americans.

Miss Hopley and her teachers never let us forget why we were at Lincoln: for those who were alien, to become good Americans; for those who were so born, to accept the rest of us. Off the school grounds we traded the same insults we heard from our elders. On the playground we were sure to be marched up to the principal's office for calling someone a wop, a chink, a dago, or a greaser. The school was not so much a melting pot as a griddle where Miss Hopley and her helpers warmed knowledge into us and roasted racial hatreds out of us.

At Lincoln, making us into Americans did not mean scrubbing away what made us originally foreign. The teachers called us as our parents did, or as close as they could pronounce our names in Spanish or Japanese. No one was ever scolded or punished for speaking his native tongue on the playground. Matti told the class about his mother's down quilt, which she had made in Italy with the fine feathers of a thousand geese. Encarnación acted out how boys learned to fish in the Philippines. I astounded the third grade with the story of my travels on a stagecoach, which nobody else in the class had seen except in the museum at Sutter's Fort. After a visit to the Crocker Art Gallery and its collection of heroic paintings of the golden age of California, someone showed a silk scroll with a Chinese painting. Miss Hopley herself had a way of expressing wonder over these matters before a class, her eyes wide open until they popped slightly. It was easy for me to feel that becoming a proud American, as she said we should, did not mean feeling ashamed of being a Mexican.

The Americanization of Mexican me was no smooth matter. I had to fight one lout who made fun of my travels on the *diligencia,* and my barbaric translation of the word into "diligence." He doubled up with laughter over the word until I straightened him out with a kick. In class I made points explaining that in Mexico roosters said "qui-qui-ri-qui" and not "cock-a-doodle-doo," but after school I had to put up with the taunts of a big Yugoslav who said Mexican roosters were crazy.

But it was Homer who gave me the most lasting lesson for a future American.

Homer was a chunky Irishman who dressed as if every day was Sunday. He slicked his hair between a crew cut and a pompadour. And Homer was smart, as he clearly showed when he and I ran for president of the third grade.

Everyone understood that this was to be a demonstration of how the American people vote for president. In an election, the teacher explained, the candidates could be generous and vote for each other. We cast our ballots in a shoe box and Homer won by two votes. I polled my supporters and came to the conclusion that I had voted for Homer and so had he. After class he didn't deny it, reminding me of what the teacher had said—we could vote for each other but didn't have to.

The lower part of town was a collage of nationalities in the middle of which Miss Nettie Hopley kept school with discipline and compassion. She called assemblies in the upper hall to introduce celebrities like the police sergeant or the fire chief, to lay down the law of the school, to present awards to our athletic champions, and to make important announcements. One of these was that I had been proposed by my school and accepted as a member of the newly formed Sacramento Boys Band. "Now, isn't that a wonderful thing?" Miss Hopley asked the assembled school, all eyes on me. And everyone answered in a chorus, including myself, "Yes, Miss Hopley."

It was not only the parents who were summoned to her office and boys and girls who served sentences there who knew that Nettie Hopley meant business. The entire school witnessed her sizzling Americanism in its awful majesty one morning at flag salute.

All the grades, as usual, were lined up in the courtyard between the wings of the building, ready to march to classes after the opening bell. Miss Shand was on the balcony of the second floor off Miss Hopley's office, conducting us in our lusty singing of "My Country tiz-a-thee." Our principal, as always, stood there like us, at attention, her right hand over her heart, joining in the song.

Halfway through the second stanza she stepped forward, held up her arm in a sign of command, and called loud and clear: "Stop the singing." Miss Shand looked flabbergasted. We were frozen with shock.

Miss Hopley was now standing at the rail of the balcony, her eyes sparking, her voice low and resonant, the words coming down to us distinctly and loaded with indignation.

"There are two gentlemen walking on the school grounds with their hats on while we are singing," she said, sweeping our ranks with her eyes. "We will remain silent until the gentlemen come to attention and remove their hats." A minute of awful silence ended when Miss Hopley, her gaze fixed on something behind us, signaled Miss Shand and we began once more the familiar hymn. That afternoon, when school was out, the word spread. The two gentlemen were the Superintendent of Schools and an important guest on an inspection.

Ernesto Galarza

☐ Ernesto describes his school life in great detail and calls the experience "the Americanization of Mexican me." Does he give indication of not being allowed to retain his Mexican heritage during this period of his life? Give examples in support of your answer.

☐ Nettie Hopley, the principal of Lincoln School, has definite goals that she wants the students to achieve. What are these goals? What do you think of them?

☐ Ernesto describes some of the ways in which the people of the barrio celebrate important events. Why are these customs so important to the Mexican-Americans? Do people in your community celebrate similar occasions? Compare customs of the barrio with ones observed in your own community.

■ ■

■ Ernesto noticed that unlike the shops, parks, and yards of Mazatlán, those of Sacramento did not encourage neighborhood activities. Look at your own neighborhood with the eye of a newcomer. Does it have places that encourage neighborhood activities? If you were chosen to propose to a town committee a design for some open areas or buildings, what would your plan be?

■ The teachers of Lincoln School tried to help the students learn to be good citizens and yet retain pride in their own cultural heritage. Discuss ways people can develop pride in their American citizenship while respecting their own and others' racial and cultural inheritances.

A Storm in Summer

*Herman, who is taking part in the
Fresh Air Vacation Plan, arrives at the
delicatessen-home of his "sponsor"—
a hardened old man who would prefer
being left alone. . . .*

> "I'm Herman D. Washington."
> "I'm Abel Shaddick."
> "I come on the train. Just a couple minutes ago."
> "I came on a boat fifty-five years ago.
> So what else should we talk about?"

Is this the beginning of a beautiful friendship?

CHARACTERS

COP	HERMAN WASHINGTON
ABEL SHADDICK	HOOD ONE
GLORIA ROSS	HOOD TWO
MRS. GOLD	MAÎTRE D'
HARRIET	MRS. PARKER
STANLEY BANNER	

ACT ONE

SCENE 1

A delicatessen in a vacation community—upstate New York. Night. We see Shaddick in the process of putting away various items—chickens, trays of cold cuts, etc. He then moves out through the front door and starts to crank up the awning. A police car pulls up to the delicatessen. A Cop gets out, checks the store, then notices Shaddick.

COP: How are you tonight, Mr. Shaddick?

SHADDICK: A day older since you last asked me.

COP: Another hot one, huh?

SHADDICK: Why not? You wanna know something? (*He jerks his thumb skyward.*) Up there—in the Kingdom of Heaven—is a special department. A Celestial Bureau dedicated to the harassment of Abel Shaddick. It is staffed by a hundred fallen angels, blueprinting my ultimate destruction.

COP (*grins*): Somebody up there doesn't like you much, huh?

SHADDICK: I can see the staff meetings now. Monday, we'll give him prickly heat. Tuesday, two bum checks he'll get and a breakdown in the refrigeration. On Wednesday, the bank will call one of his notes, and on Thursday, his nephew Stanley will come to stay with him. And on Friday—which is today—they'll send down a heat wave. We'll give him ninety-eight degrees—with humidity, yet—so he'll have insomnia' and have to lie in bed all night worrying about something worse than Friday.

COP (*grins*): What's worse than Friday?

SHADDICK: Saturday!

SCENE 2

The next morning, bright and sunny. Shaddick starts to lower the old awning, letting it squeak slowly down. At one point,

87

while he's turning the handle, it sticks. This is obviously an everyday occurrence. He gives the handle a slap with his hand to free it, and the awning continues down into place. Shaddick enters the delicatessen carrying crates. The delicatessen is a dark little cubicle of a place with long antiquated counter, a few sad-looking chickens hanging on hooks, some salamis, a pickle barrel, a hotplate alongside a chopping block . . . and finally a picture of a young air force lieutenant.

SHADDICK: Morning, Benjy. (*The phone rings. Shaddick picks up the receiver.*) Yes? (*Takes pencil and pad of paper.*) One pint pickled herrings. Yes. Loaf of corn rye. You want that sliced? All right. (*Pause.*) Yes, lady—I'm writing it down. A Chinese waiter I'm not! (*Continues to scribble down order.*) Yes. Two dozen eggs. That it? (*Pause.*) No, lady—I don't deliver. I'm too poor for a truck and too old for a bicycle! (*He furiously scrawls out everything he's written.*) So suit yourself. You wanna come in and pick it up—come in and pick it up. (*Pause.*) That's right, lady—independent! (*Slams down the phone, stares at it, shakes head. Then, aloud to himself.*) Deliveries yet. Food stamps. Lucky numbers. Name the President. Hit the jackpot. A black year on the Twentieth Century! (*He goes behind the counter, moves over to the picture of his son, looks at it.*) So, Benjy—the hot spell continues. Your cousin Stanley has been here for six days—oh, I told you yesterday. And your cousin Stanley, as I also told you, has all the charm of an untipped waiter. He commutes between his mattress and the Country Club. And should I have failed to mention it, Benjy—your cousin Stanley is not my glass of tea.

A Cadillac convertible pulls up in front of the store. Gloria Ross, a tall, long-legged, stunning blonde, gets out of the car, looks a little dubiously at the store front, and then enters. A bell rings.

SHADDICK: Can I help you, lady?
GLORIA (*brittle smile—half nervous, half condescension*): Good morning. . . . Does a Mr. Banner live here?
SHADDICK: Mr. Banner? Oh yes, Mr. Banner. Formerly Mr. "Bloom." Strictly speaking, he doesn't *live* here. He just

drops in on occasion in between his big deals. Mr. Banner, formerly Mr. Bloom, is my nephew.

GLORIA (*smile persists*): You must be Mr. Shaddick.

SHADDICK: I must be. . . . Now what can I get you?

GLORIA (*removes papers from her purse*): I'm Gloria Ross, Mr. Shaddick. I met your nephew at the Club last night.

Slight pause as Shaddick glares at her. Her smile fades slightly.

GLORIA: The Country Club. Perhaps Mister . . . Mr. Banner mentioned it.

SHADDICK: By the time my nephew with the new name returned to his mattress early this morning, I'd already had five hours of sleep and two sizable nightmares—one having to do with an avenging angel knocking on my door and telling me that Stanley Banner, formerly Bloom, would live with me for the rest of his life. (*Pause.*) No, lady—I have not talked to my nephew since early yesterday.

The bell rings again. A little old lady waddles in—Mrs. Gold—a "professional shopper," a chicken feeler, pickle analyst, and all-round pain.

MRS. GOLD: Morning, Shaddick.

Shaddick mumbles. She starts feeling vegetables, then heads toward a line of plucked chickens hanging in scrawny, post-mortem inactivity and immediately begins to feel them, one by one. Shaddick throws her one icy look, then turns back toward Gloria.

GLORIA: (*Her smile persists, but it's wearing around the edges.*) You've no doubt heard of the Fresh Air Vacation Plan—

SHADDICK (*another look at Mrs. Gold fingering the chickens*): The Fresh Air Vacation Plan.

GLORIA (*eagerly*): We bring children in from the city to spend two weeks here with families in the community. But of course . . . well . . . we make it a policy to check on the nature of the homes that the children are entering. It's just a . . . a standard procedure. You know, just to make certain of . . . of compatibility.

SHADDICK: So how much does my nephew Stanley owe for the raffle tickets?

GLORIA (*frowning a little*): No, there aren't any raffle tickets, Mr. Shaddick. You see, when a family volunteers to take a child—

SHADDICK (*interrupting by turning away, pointing toward Mrs. Gold*): Mrs. Gold—you here to purchase or just fondle?

MRS. GOLD (*icy disdain*): I don't buy anything but the fresh. (*She points to the chickens.*) These are fresh?

SHADDICK: They were until you potchkeyed with them.

MRS. GOLD: You want my business or don't you, Mr. Shaddick?

SHADDICK: Your business I would welcome, Mrs. Gold—but your daily rubdown of my poultry I can do without.

MRS. GOLD: I'll take this one. (*Brings it to Shaddick.*)

SHADDICK: A prize-winner . . . lucky chicken . . . I found a home for you.

He throws it on the scale. Mrs. Gold peers over the counter to check the weight.

MRS. GOLD: Just the chicken, Mr. Shaddick—I'm not buying your thumb.

Shaddick throws her a disdainful, icy look, scoops the chicken off the scale, tosses it on some brown paper, wraps it up deftly, ties it up, bites off the string, tosses it on the counter.

SHADDICK: A dollar ninety-one.

Mrs. Gold laboriously counts out change, puts it on the counter, takes the chicken, stares back at Shaddick.

MRS. GOLD: If it's no good, you'll hear from me.

SHADDICK (*nodding*): I won't sleep until your decision is handed down.

Mrs. Gold walks haughtily toward the door, mumbling, moves out, slamming it behind her. Shaddick nods, hot with anger, tight-lipped.

SHADDICK: Some way to start a day—protecting the honor of a plucked chicken. (*Turns to Gloria.*) Nu?

GLORIA (*nervous, flustered, ill at ease*): Do you think I could speak to Stanley—?

SHADDICK: The big shot? Like I told you—he's in the sack.

GLORIA (*taking the bit in her teeth*): The child is supposed to arrive today, Mr. Shaddick—

SHADDICK: What child?

GLORIA: I've been trying to explain it to you. Mr. Banner—Mr. Bloom—your nephew Stanley—he volunteered—

SHADDICK (*interrupting her*): He volunteered? A child is coming here because my nephew Stanley volunteered? Lady, if Hermann Goering had a child—I wouldn't wish him on my nephew. Now if you want to bring a boy here and turn him into a delinquent—you'll find there the greatest instructor since Fagin!

GLORIA: You still don't understand, Mr. Shaddick.

SHADDICK (*throwing up his hands, his voice loud*): What, what, what? Tell me. What don't I understand?

GLORIA (*almost recoiling*): The idea was that you'd be, in a sense, co-sponsors of the child. Stanley assured us that he'd be staying with you through the summer—

He whirls around, picks up a cleaver off the chopping block. Gloria hurriedly moves back a foot. Shaddick whirls around toward her, holding the cleaver.

SHADDICK: Lady from the Country Club—do yourself a favor! The next time my big-shot nephew shows up at one of your pishy-poshy Junior League affairs, just show him the door and the restricted clause in the Club Constitution.

GLORIA: Really, Mr. Shaddick—

SHADDICK (*overlapping her*): That way you'll save yourself embarrassment and very likely a bum check. Good-bye, lady.

The girl stands there, blinking, and it takes a moment for anything to come out.

GLORIA: What . . . what about the boy? He's probably on a train by now.

SHADDICK: Then take him *off* the train.

GLORIA: (*For the first time, anger overcomes fear.*) Mr. Shaddick, a little child is coming here out of the slums—

SHADDICK (*disgusted*): Please, lady—that's where *I* came from, and I still don't get enough fresh air. (*Jerks his thumb in the direction of the stairway.*) All I got is that freeloader in the summer tuxedo up there—half sponge, half mouth!

GLORIA: Mr. Shaddick . . .

SHADDICK: You go back and tell your members that I got no time for children, no sympathy for their social charities, and no place for my nephew Stanley Banner! This is my final word! Again—good-bye, lady! (*Turns his back on her, walks away.*)

GLORIA: You've put me in a dreadful position, Mr. Shaddick. I'm going to be on the phone half the day trying to . . .

SHADDICK: Lady, please, enough already. (*He stands there listening to her footsteps as she leaves. The bell rings when the door closes.*)

Gloria leaves the delicatessen and walks over to her convertible. Another debutante type sits alongside the driver's seat. She looks expectantly toward Gloria, who comes around and enters through the driver's door.

HARRIET: What's he like?

GLORIA (*turns on the ignition*): Scrooge, from the East Side! (*Throws the car into gear.*) You put some poor unsuspecting little kid in with that bilious old goat, he'd be scarred for life.

HARRIET: That kid may be on a train now.

GLORIA: I'll put in a call to New York.

Harriet takes a piece of paper out of her purse, looks up.

HARRIET: The kid's name is Washington.

GLORIA: As in George.

HARRIET (*with a little smile, shakes her head*): Not according to this. As in Booker T.

The car zooms away from the curb.

SCENE 3

Inside the delicatessen. Stanley starts down the steps. He is a two-bit sharpy in mod with a surface veneer of gall. He comes down the steps à la Fred Astaire, singing and finger-snapping —and once down, moves over to the hotplate and a mug of coffee. The dance steps and the singing continue. Shaddick looks skyward at the invisible God.

STANLEY: Morning, Unc . . . .

SHADDICK (*to himself*): Tell me something—I deserve this?

STANLEY: Nice affair at the Club last night.

Shaddick just glares at him, then turns his back.

STANLEY: Gonna be hot today. New York'll be murder. (*Pause.*) I gotta be there by lunchtime. (*Another pause; still no response from Shaddick.*) Guy I know got a discotheque in Atlantic City. He's lookin' for a manager. Could be three bills a week and a cut. (*He moves to Shaddick. Now his mission in life is to get a rise out of his uncle.*) Unc. How does that grab you?

SHADDICK: Me it doesn't grab so much. But the Atlantic City Vice Squad—give them a message for me, Stanley. They put you away for more than sixty days . . . I'll send them free salami!

STANLEY: My uncle, the sentimentalist! Listen, I could be gone for quite some time—

SHADDICK: I'm destitute.

STANLEY (*shakes his head, grins at him*): I'll bet. Well, I'll send you a postcard from Atlantic City—

SHADDICK: I already know Atlantic City. And your postcards usually cost me two cents to cover the insufficient postage. Do me a favor, Stanley—if by some miracle you get the job and the three bills a week, and you find yourself with an extra ten bucks, please use 'em to buy some flowers for your mama's grave.

STANLEY (*looks at him, smile fading*): You got a thing about death, don't you, Unc?

SHADDICK: You don't, huh, Stanley? You're immortal. You don't die.

Stanley tilts his head at him—half bemused, half not really liking the old man or understanding him.

STANLEY: How long has Ben been gone? Nineteen forty-four, wasn't it? That's almost twenty-five years ago. You keep his picture around . . . his effects . . . like he was killed on Thursday.

SHADDICK: Mr. Bloom—son of my late sister—my bed you can borrow. My telephone you can use. My food, feel free to eat . . . but how I mourn my child . . . and for how long . . . that's *my* business. Understand?

STANLEY (*with an exaggerated shrug*): All right, all right! (*Looks at his watch, whistles.*) Oh, look at the time! I wanna catch the eleven o'clock train. . . . Stay loose, Unc.

Stanley starts through the door. Shaddick holds up a hand.

SHADDICK: A moment, please, Mr. Rockefeller. An item of unfinished business. Namely, your latest philanthropy.

STANLEY (*turns to him from the door and frowns*): What're you talking about?

SHADDICK: The slum child you're going to entertain for two weeks. A lady was here earlier. Miss Ross.

STANLEY (*slaps his palm against his forehead*): I forgot all about that. . . . I'll call her from the station.

SHADDICK: You do that, Stanley; your bad debts I'll meet—your indiscriminate charities—No!

STANLEY: Relax! Will you relax? (*Thin little smile.*) I got a little high last night. They had this booth where they were signing up kids—they had one more to place—well, you know how it is.

SHADDICK (*unsmiling*): I know how it is with *you*. A good deed must be accompanied by a brass section and a photographer!

STANELY: How is it with you, Unc?

SHADDICK: Yeah. . . . Explain the question?

STANLEY: I don't know how you survive.

SHADDICK: I manage.

STANLEY: What do you manage? Seven days a week, hating everything you do and doing the same thing. Up at eight, open the cases, hang up the chickens, scream at somebody

94

on the phone. Nine o'clock at night you lock it all up, and next morning you start all over again.

SHADDICK: In the parlance of the time, Stanley, that's what's known as making a living. Easy it's not. Enjoyable it's not. But it's what ancient idiots like me do to stay alive. I wouldn't expect *you* to understand it. Anyone who could change a name like they change their shirt—this kind of person wants the rose without the thorn. Life isn't like that! Life is misery. But *I* made a pact with it.

STANLEY: You made a pact with it; you love it. Because that's the way you're built, Unc. You'd rather be caught dead than smiling.

SHADDICK: You wanna see me smile, Stanley? In heaven, you'll see me smile. When they read out my will and they get to that part where it says how much I leave to my nephew, Stanley Banner. One blank page.

STANLEY (*shakes his head back and forth and has to smile*): I can't top you, Unc. I'll go pack. (*Starts toward stairs.*) Wish me luck.

SHADDICK (*shrugs*): What I wish for you, I apologize to God for.

SCENE 4

A small train station. The train is just pulling out. The room is mobbed with fresh-air kids, all tagged and identified. They are led away by waiting foster parents. Herman Washington stands by himself—a grim little gnome—a tiny man-child in an altogether unpromising land. Stanley enters, moves over to the ticket cage, buys a ticket, turns, spots Herman sitting alone, reacts. Stanley moves to Herman. Looks briefly at the name tag and sees his own name underneath.

STANLEY: Whadd'ya say?

HERMAN (*looks at him very soberly*): You the man what they call the sponsor?

STANLEY (*wetting his lips a little nervously*): I'm Stan Banner. You're . . . (*reads from the tag*) . . . Herman Washington.

HERMAN (*nods*): Where we goin'?

STANLEY (*nervous falsetto laugh*): We got a little problem—

(*Herman waits patiently*). Like here I've been waiting for you all along—and suddenly I get this special hurry-up call to get to New York. (*Herman again just waits and doesn't respond.*) But I tell you what you do. You go down to the delicatessen—it's just down the street—turn right out there and you'll run right into it. A little tiny place on the other side of the street. My uncle's there. He'll look after you until I get back.

LOUDSPEAKER VOICE: Eleven-oh-eight to New York now arriving.

STANLEY: That's my train, kid. (*Sticks out his hand.*) You have a ball, Herm. I'll be seeing you later.

Herman looks at the hand, then very slowly lets his eyes rise up to Stanley's face, making his own very special inventory.

STANLEY (*moves to the ticket window*): New York. . . . (*Turns to Herman.*) Don't let my uncle turn you off. He's not a bad egg. Just a little . . . a little old and . . . set in his ways. . . . But you go over there and tell him who you are.

Herman picks up his battered laundry case, looks toward the door, then back to Stanley.

STANLEY (*hung-up, guilty, and anxious*): I'm awful sorry I gotta cut out on you like this, Herm. I mean it.

HERMAN: Your uncle like you?

STANLEY (*blinks*): You don't dig me?

HERMAN (*after slow headshake*): You talk too much and you talk too loud.

Herman turns and moves to the door, leaving Stanley there just blinking at him. He leaves carrying his laundry case and starts at a slow walk down the sidewalk toward the heart of town.

SCENE 5

Inside the delicatessen. Shaddick finishes arranging trays inside the display case, then looks up toward the window. Stand-

*ing on the sidewalk, staring back at him, is Herman—the un-
dersized black militant with a grim, set, determined, chal-
lenging look on his face. There's no question that he's right out
of a ghetto. And this moment finds him out of it for the first
time. He has to exercise his own special brand of courage to com-
bat his fear. After a moment he straightens his shoulders, moves
into the delicatessen, reading from a paper in his hand as he
does so. Shaddick at this point doesn't make the connection at all
between his nephew and the child.*

SHADDICK (*after long, waiting pause*): Nu?

HERMAN (*blinks, frowns, looks down at himself*): You mean the
suit?

SHADDICK: I mean—what can I get you?

HERMAN (*puts down the laundry case*): What do you got?

SHADDICK: What do you want?

HERMAN: Got a Coca-Cola?

SHADDICK: For a Coca-Cola, you go to the drugstore.

HERMAN: I'll take a glass of water.

SHADDICK: A glass of water. (*Shrugs, moves over to the sink,
rinses out the glass, carries it back over to the counter, puts
the glass on top of it.*) With customers like you I could go
bankrupt in a week. Here you are. . . .

*Herman reaches up for the glass, takes it, drinks thirstily, re-
turns it to the top of the counter. He stands there, unsure of himself for a moment, then fingers a large hand-painted badge on
his lapel which reads, "Herman D. Washington."*

HERMAN: I'm Herman D. Washington.

SHADDICK: I'm Abel Shaddick. . . .

HERMAN: I come on the train. Just a couple minutes ago.

SHADDICK (*scratches his head, leans on the counter*): I came on a
boat fifty-five years ago. So what else should we talk
about?

HERMAN: This here is the address I was supposed to go to, so I'm
your kid.

SHADDICK: Mr. Washington, do you get the same impression

that I do—that there is occurring a breakdown in our communication?

HERMAN (*studying him*): Don't you dig, man? . . . I'm supposed to stay here two weeks. (*He looks down at a piece of paper.*) Stanley Banner. (*He looks up.*) He's what they call my sponsor. He was at the train station. He sent me here. (*The light dawns on Shaddick.*) My Gramma got this phone call late last night. Lady say I should be on the train at eight o'clock. So that's what I done. (*Holds up the paper in his hand.*) And they give me this here thing to tell me who was gonna meet me. And where I was supposed to go. That Stanley cat—the one I met—he say I should come over here and see you.

SHADDICK (*hesitates*): Mr. Washington. . . . The man you accurately described as the Stanley cat, Mr. Banner, has left town and in the process left both of us on a limb. I'm afraid that . . . that . . . well, there is nobody here to look after you.

Herman nods. His brief eight years have obviously been a parade of disappointments. He assimilates them like food. He reaches into his pocket, his face sober, takes out a train ticket, puts it on the counter.

HERMAN: Is this what I use to go back to New York?

SHADDICK (*turns it around and looks at it, nods*): That's right. It's the return part of your ticket. Don't lose that now. (*Looks up at the clock on the wall.*) The next train is about three hours from now. You've missed the eleven o'clock.

HERMAN: Okay. (*He looks, fascinated, at the counter.*)

SHADDICK (*very reluctantly*): You want some breakfast? (*Pause.*) I asked you a question. Do you want some breakfast? You want something to eat?

Herman, after studying Shaddick intensely, shakes his head.

HERMAN: I jus' go back on the train. I don't wanna stay here.

SHADDICK (*shrugs, vaguely disturbed, but not sure why*): So go back on the train. But first—the least I could do is offer you something to eat. . . . See anything you like?

Herman takes a slow walk down the length of the counter, looking into the display case.

HERMAN (*pointing*): What's that there?

SHADDICK: Show me. . . . That's pastrami. You want a nice pastrami sandwich?

HERMAN: What's pastrami?

SHADDICK: It's corned beef. Highly seasoned. It's . . . it's Jewish.

HERMAN (*looks up at him*): You Jewish?

SHADDICK: I don't look Jewish—right?

HERMAN: Guy who own our building—he Jewish. Man, he a pretty bad cat. Nobody likes him. I ain't hungry. (*Turns toward the door.*)

SHADDICK: So where are you going?

HERMAN: To the train station.

SHADDICK: You got a three-hour wait. You might as well stay here. (*Herman shakes his head.*) Why not?

HERMAN: 'Cause I don't like you.

SHADDICK (*again disturbed but unable to put his finger on why*): So you don't like me. So go sit in a hot train station and broil for three hours.

HERMAN: What you care?

SHADDICK: I don't care. I really don't care. Between a bankrupt business and a bum nephew, I don't need a three-foot-tall Ethiopian anti-Semite! You, I don't need.

Shaddick deliberately turns his back on the boy. Herman looks through the glass of the display case to a tray of fish. Shaddick turns toward him.

SHADDICK: Nu? What keeps you?

HERMAN (*pointing toward the fish*): Them are fish.

SHADDICK: That's what them are.

HERMAN (*looks up at him*): I never been fishin'. They told me that's one of the things you done when you got sponsored. People take you fishin'. (*Looks down at the fish.*) I ain't never been fishin'.

Shaddick moves down the counter, leans on it, looking across and down at the boy.

SHADDICK: Where do you live?

HERMAN: 136th Street.

SHADDICK (*softly*): No lakes on 136th Street, huh?

HERMAN (*shakes his head, then looks up*): You got a lake here?

SHADDICK: Yeah, I got a small lake.

HERMAN: You ever fish in it?

SHADDICK: My son and I used to. My son. Now there was a fisherman. (*Moves over to the picture, holds it up.*) That's him there . . . Benjy.

HERMAN: Soljer.

SHADDICK: Second lieutenant. A bombardier.

HERMAN: Where is he now?

SHADDICK (*with a soft little smile*): He was killed on a raid over a place called Stuttgart.

HERMAN: I got a brother. His name's Bill. He's in Vietnam. A sergeant. Man, he's a tiger. He sent me a picture of him carryin' a gun. He's a real tiger. (*Looks intently at the picture, then into Shaddick's face.*) You say he's dead?

SHADDICK (*nods*): He was nineteen. (*Looks at the picture.*) This was twenty-four years ago.

HERMAN: What about your mama? (*Then, frowning.*) I mean, *his* mama.

SHADDICK: His mama died many years ago when he was a baby. I raised him.

HERMAN (*studies Shaddick intently*): Who is this cat Stanley?

SHADDICK: Don't ask. (*Looks long at the boy.*) Thanks to him, you took a train ride for nothing.

HERMAN: Where this here lake?

SHADDICK: You want to see the lake? It's one mile south. You take a left on Main Street. Lake Wanateeshie.

HERMAN (*repeating it but stumbling*): Wana-tee-shie. (*Frowns.*) That Jewish?

SHADDICK: Jewish-Indian. While you're gone, I'll call the lady here in town who's responsible for you. She can phone your grandmother. (*Turns away, busying himself behind the counter.*) All right, go along then and . . . don't drown.

HERMAN: When my brother come back—he gonna take me fishin'. He promise me. My brother—when he say somethin', you gotta believe him.

100

SHADDICK (*nods*): Without question. It's a trait that runs in your family. Honor and invincibility.

Herman remains standing there. A pause.

SHADDICK: So what do you wait for now—the Messiah?

HERMAN: This here lake I'm goin' to—nobody gonna give me trouble—is they? I mean . . . I mean . . . I'm black.

SHADDICK: Who could give you trouble? Who would dare? You're the only ten-year-old kid on earth who sounds like Humphrey Bogart. (*He turns to Herman who still stands there, unsure, irresolute.*) Now what?

HERMAN: Nothin'.

SHADDICK: Nothin'. That means *something*.

HERMAN: That mean *nothin'*.

SHADDICK: You're afraid to tell me?

HERMAN: Afraid? No way, baby. No how.

SHADDICK: Then speak your mind, why don't you?

HERMAN (*after a pause*): Don't *you* ever go fishin'?

SHADDICK: Not since my Benjy was killed have I put a worm to hook. . . . Why?

HERMAN: Nothin'.

SHADDICK: Nothing, meaning why don't you and I go fishing?

Herman shrugs but doesn't say anything. Shaddick looks at Benjy.

SHADDICK: Benjy . . . an inspiration! (*He whirls around, pounds a fist on the cash register to ring up a "no sale."*) Since the first of the month I haven't taken in enough to pay the electric bill—and this fisherman from 136th Street thinks I got nothing better in life to do than play Huckleberry Finn.

Herman stares at him. Shaddick returns the look.

HERMAN: What that thing you say goes runnin' in the family?

SHADDICK (*frowning*): A trait.

HERMAN (*nods*): Whatever you call it. You got the same thing goin' between Stanley and you.

SHADDICK (*sardonically*): The itinerant philosopher. So tell me. What is the trait that binds me with my nephew Stanley?

HERMAN (*emotionlessly*): You're the same kinda cats. He get on a train. You hide behind the pastrami.

Shaddick gnaws slightly on his lower lip, studying the boy, then the delicatessen. Then he looks up toward the clock.

SHADDICK: You know what an Achilles' Heel is? (*Herman shakes his head.*) It's an infected boil on the soul. (*Again he looks up toward the clock. Then he starts to remove his apron.*) For maybe an hour I'll go with you. But for no longer than an hour.

HERMAN: Maybe we gonna catch some big fish; then you can sell 'em.

SHADDICK: Mr. Washington . . . with my luck I will catch one minnow, one sunstroke, and a summons from the Game Warden.

He heaves a gigantic sigh, moves to the door, opens it and hangs up the "Closed" sign. Herman stands in the doorway holding his suitcase.

SHADDICK: A question: In your luggage there . . . you got worms? (*Herman shakes his head.*) Then why are you taking it with us?

Herman leaves the suitcase inside by the door. Shaddick looks down at Herman, who gives him a quizzical look.

SHADDICK: Nu? You got something to say?

HERMAN: You forgot somethin'.

SHADDICK: Enlighten me.

HERMAN: Fishin' poles. We ain't got no fishin' poles. When you go fishin', you gotta have fishin' poles.

SHADDICK (*nods seriously as if responding to some incredibly deep philosophy*): I give you this, Herman. You have all the gaiety of an undertaker—but you are a very discerning boy. Very discerning. So you know what we'll have to do? We'll have to stop at the hardware store, and we'll buy what was it?

HERMAN: Fishing poles.

They start down the sidewalk. Every now and then Herman

102

looks a little secretively at Shaddick. They stop at a light before crossing the street.

SHADDICK: Ah . . . I need this. (*Shaddick reaches down to take the boy's hand. Herman pulls it away.*) That's to cross the street.

HERMAN (*quite seriously*): I been crossin' streets since I was two years old.

SHADDICK (*looks down at him*): I don't suppose it ever occurred to you that maybe I needed help crossing the street?

HERMAN (*nods very seriously*): That's different, man. (*He looks up at Shaddick's hand, frowns.*) What you say your name was?

SHADDICK: Shaddick. Abel Shaddick. (*Herman looks very thoughtful.*) You don't like it?

HERMAN (*shrugs*): Makes no difference to me what they call you.

The signal light turns green. Herman reaches up, takes Shaddick's hand.

HERMAN: Let's go, Shaddick.

SHADDICK (*for the first time, smiling*): I'm right with you, Washington.

They walk across the street hand in hand.

ACT TWO

SCENE 1

Shaddick and Herman are perched on a large jutting rock that overhangs the lake. They both have fishing poles. Shaddick is explaining how to use them.

SHADDICK: Now this is what you have to do, Herman. Keep your eye on that bobbin. The bait we are using, Herman, is what the fish want.

HERMAN: Why?

SHADDICK (*blinks at him for a moment*): Because . . . because a wise fish knows what he wants. Every once in a while give the line a little pull.

HERMAN (*imitating him*): Like this?

SHADDICK: Just a little bit . . . that's it. If we're lucky, this will attract their attention. Now when the fish nibbles, the bobbin will begin to shake. And when that happens, don't get excited. When he's got the hook in his mouth, he'll pull the bobbin way underwater. Then you give it a good tug and that sets the hook. You understand me? (*Herman nods.*) Now I, myself, have conquered this thing only in theory. But my son, Benjy . . . there was a fisherman. He had a nose for it.

HERMAN: A nose?

SHADDICK: An instinct. (*Shakes his head back and forth.*) Right from the start I never had to teach Benjy anything.

While Shaddick is talking, Herman sees that there is a fish on Shaddick's line. Shaddick continues to talk, unaware of what's going on.

SHADDICK: I remember one summer—lessee—it must have been around '37, '38 . . . in that area but a little further down. . . . Benjy caught a bass at this very lake. . . . (*Herman tugs at him.*) Such a bass. . . . (*Pauses, shuts his eyes, still oblivious to the boy tugging at him.*) All I know is that this was a fish among fish—

105

HERMAN (*exploding*): You got somethin', man! You got a fish! Somethin's pullin'—

SHADDICK: What did I tell you to do?! Remind me!

Shaddick is suddenly aware of what is going on, rises, and topples forward with a yell into the shallow water below. He sits in the water, drenched—water up around his neck. Herman has gotten his own bite and is pulling furiously on his line, reeling in as he pulls. A large bass emerges on Herman's line. He pulls it off the hook and then holds it, squirming in his hand.

HERMAN: Look! Hey, man! I gotta fish! Look at this! This here a real fish, ain't it! And I got it! Ain't this some fish?

Shaddick is sitting in the water, his rod and reel floating nearby. He looks up at Herman on the rock, wipes his wet face with a sleeve—tries to interrupt Herman.)

SHADDICK: I see the fish. . . . Mr. Washington—a favor? (*Herman, still clutching the fish, looks down at him.*) You have one more minute to exult in pulling in the fish. After that, be so kind as to pull in this ancient mariner.

Herman carefully puts the fish in a cheap basket alongside, then climbs down from the rock, wades out to where Shaddick is, and helps the old man to shore.

SCENE 2

Inside the delicatessen. Night. Shaddick enters from the bedroom. Herman is asleep on the bed, dead to the world. On the table is a plate of partially eaten food and an empty glass. Shaddick picks up the plate and glass, turns and walks out of the room with them. He starts to wash the dishes, looks at the picture.

SHADDICK: Benjy—today, a revelation! I now know what ultimately destroys old men. It is not hardening of the arteries, as has been thought—but a softening of the brain. Inside my bedroom, sleeping, is a small dark shadow with a chip on his shoulder the size of a loaf of pumpernickel! And you know what I've been doing today, Benjy? I've been fishing on the lake with this boy. Where you and I used to go. Five and a half hours in the hot sun—much of it spent underwater—because your cousin Stanley has got a mouth like a whale and the instincts of a shark!

A car pulls up in front of the delicatessen. Gloria Ross gets out of the convertible, leaving an attractive young man on the front seat. She walks toward the door, opens it. The bell rings.

GLORIA: I received a message you'd called, Mr. Shaddick—

SHADDICK: It was so long ago, I'd forgotten.

GLORIA (*with courteous apology*): I'm so sorry. It was the golf tournament—

SHADDICK: Miss Ross, for each day of your life I wish you a hole-in-one. But at the moment, I've got a few problems of my own.

GLORIA: I understand from your message that the little boy arrived and he's here with you.

SHADDICK (*with a jerk of his thumb toward the bedroom*): He's asleep.

GLORIA: Didn't your nephew—

SHADDICK (*interrupting*): Don't mention that name, please. Now did you find someone else in town who can take the child off my hands?

GLORIA: That's why I'm here, Mr. Shaddick. I'm going to have to take the child myself.

SHADDICK: He'll make a good caddy.

GLORIA: Well, he obviously can't stay here.

SHADDICK: For once, we're in agreement. Between a seventy-two-year-old Jew and a ten-year-old black boy, Miss Ross, there is not what you would call a mutuality of interest.

GLORIA: He can stay with me tonight, and I'll arrange to send him home in the morning.

SHADDICK: Home? Are you telling me that on the membership rolls of that pishy-poshy Club of yours, there isn't one lousy family willing to take him?

GLORIA: Given time, we'd find many. (*An apologetic smile.*) But we want the boy to feel comfortable. And under the circumstances—well . . . you know—

SHADDICK (*intensely*): Enlighten me.

GLORIA: Well, for a black child to move into—

SHADDICK: A black child.

GLORIA: Now wait a minute. . . .

SHADDICK: The cardinal sin.

GLORIA (*tightly*): Don't make me out a bigot—

SHADDICK (*interrupting her*): Then don't make *me* out an idiot! I'm a long time on this earth, lady—and I'm an expert on bigotry.

GLORIA (*struggling for composure and patience*): Mr. Shaddick, I want that little boy to enjoy himself. I don't care what color he is. But you don't take a child off a Harlem street, stick him in a swimming pool at the Country Club, and expect him to make an adjustment between breakfast and lunch!

SHADDICK: Since when is swimming such an adjustment?

GLORIA: This is a sociological problem.

SHADDICK: *Mazel tov*[1] to all the sociological problems in the world. I got a feeling about you, Miss Ross . . . you'll forgive me in advance . . . that you dabble in good deeds the way a person would reach for a pickle in a barrel. Tentatively and gingerly.

GLORIA: I think that will be quite enough, Mr. Shaddick.

SHADDICK: Not quite. You're a little like my nephew. You're so busy dressing up for the Charity Ball—you forget what the Charity is! An act of kindness, Miss Ross, is not such a big deal when it comes in fashionable spasms during the social season! You understand!

GLORIA: I'll take the boy now, Mr. Shaddick.

SHADDICK: Miss Ross, you shouldn't give yourself such trouble. The boy . . . stays here. Maybe two days . . . maybe a week.

GLORIA (*letting it all out*): That's very nice, Mr. Shaddick. Well, let me tell you something. You don't like my good deeds—I don't like yours. They're grudging, rotten-tempered afterthoughts, using a child you couldn't care less about as a gesture to those of us you loathe. And I gather you loathe a lot of us, Mr. Shaddick.

---

[1] *Mazel tov* (mä′zl tôf)

SHADDICK: Which is my right, Miss Ross?

GLORIA: Yes, it is, Mr. Shaddick. And it proves the point. You don't have to go to a country club to find a bigot—sometimes they're in delicatessens.

Shaddick's head goes down for a moment as the words hit him, and also their elementary truth. Then he looks up, half smiles.

SHADDICK: So we each drew a little blood—Miss Ross? (*Pause. He looks back toward the curtained partition, then back to Gloria.*) But the boy stays here . . . and we'll do a little fishing . . . a little hiking . . . maybe even compare notes on ghettoes. I am not the most gracious of men, Miss Ross —as you have pointed out. But in my life I have made some friends.

GLORIA: Good night, Mr. Shaddick.

She nods, turns, opens the door, and goes out. The door slams and the bell tinkles loudly. Herman comes out, rubbing his eyes with one hand, holding the fish in the other.

SHADDICK: Nu? (*Points to the fish.*) You got plans for that?

HERMAN (*nods*): What did the lady want?

SHADDICK: She wanted to divest herself of responsibility. This is the national pastime, Herman. The great American sport. This year's slogan: "Let George do it."

HERMAN: Who's George?

SHADDICK: George. Tom, Dick, and Harry. Somebody else. The other guy. I play the game too.

HERMAN (*cocking his head at him*): You sure do talk funny.

SHADDICK: What are you going to do with that?

HERMAN: I gonna get it stuffed. And then I gonna put one of them metal things with writing on it underneath—

SHADDICK: A plaque.

HERMAN (*delighted*): Yeah, a plaque. And I gonna say on it, "This fish caught by Herman D. Washington in honor of his brother Bill—sergeant in the Green Berets . . . with love from his brother, Herman D. Washington." (*Looks up, suddenly concerned.*) Can I get that all in there?

SHADDICK: In small print.

HERMAN (*holds up the fish*): Big, ain't she?

SHADDICK: Enormous. (*Moves over to the fish, takes it from Herman.*) But we'll put it on ice so that by the time it reaches your brother, he'll be able to stand close enough to read the small print. (*Shaddick carries the fish to the cooler, opens it, puts the fish on the shelf, looks at the box.*) Herman, I want to ask you something. You have a choice. You can leave on the train tomorrow morning, or you can stay here with me for a few days.

HERMAN: Why?

SHADDICK: What do you mean, why?

HERMAN: Why you want me to stay?

SHADDICK: Did I say I wanted you to stay? I gave you a choice. I said you could stay if you wanted to, or you could go home tomorrow.

HERMAN (*as always, analyzing, in his little-old-man way—and dead serious*): I'm gonna stay a coupla days.

SHADDICK (*with a gesture*): I'm overwhelmed. (*Pause.*) Now go wash your face and hands in that sink there . . . been touching fish. . . . Then we'll go see what's playing at the movies. And then after that we'll have a soda. And after that we'll come back here and I'll lie awake half the night wondering why I'm going to all the trouble. (*Shaddick watches him, amused.*)

HERMAN (*looking at Shaddick*): You lookin' at me all smiley. Why you look at me smiley?

SHADDICK: You prefer rage?

HERMAN: You know what my brother Bill say? He say he don't care if Mister Charlie hates him . . . and he sure as hell don't care if Mister Charlie likes him. He say that Mister Charlie should just get his foot offa him. That what my brother Bill say.

SHADDICK (*reacting*): Have I put my foot on you?

HERMAN: I just wanted to tell you. I'm stayin' because it hot in New York. And here I can go fishin'. That why I'm stayin'. (*Crosses to the bedroom. Shaddick follows him.*) Too bad you ain't black.

SHADDICK: Why?

HERMAN: I seen all the people lookin' at us this afternoon while we was fishin'.

SHADDICK: So they looked at us.

HERMAN: I know what they thinkin'.

SHADDICK: Enlighten me.

HERMAN: They thinkin' . . . they thinkin', "What that li'l black boy doin' with the old Jew?"

Shaddick's face turns grim and cold. He walks over to Herman.

SHADDICK: Listen, as one former ghetto dweller to another—a lesson maybe both of us should learn, Herman. Once two people go fishing together . . . or to the movies . . . all they should care about is that they enjoy. This is fundamental.

HERMAN (*looks up at him*): We equal, huh?

SHADDICK: More than we both realize.

HERMAN: There's rats where I live. Great big ones. And the johns stink. You smell 'em all over the building. If we equal—how come I gotta live there? (*His mind gallops ahead.*) When my brother come back, we gonna move outta there. We gonna move out to the country. (*Stares straight at Shaddick.*) And we gonna spit right in that Jew landlord's eye. (*Shaddick winces at this.*)

SHADDICK (*voice soft, almost a whisper*): *Mazel tov.* But for the time being . . . with *this* Jew . . . you'll go to the movies.

HERMAN (*shrugs*): Okay.

SHADDICK: The good fortune of Abel Shaddick. A hundred and seventy million people I could have as a house guest . . . and I get this midget Gamal Nasser of Harlem!

Herman follows Shaddick to the door. Shaddick flicks a light switch, then opens the door. Herman goes out, reaches for the "Closed" sign, hangs it on the doorknob outside. Shaddick closes the door and locks it.

SCENE 3

Ice cream parlor. Shaddick and Herman are sitting in a near-empty room, finishing up two sodas.

111

HERMAN: . . . but when the cat with the machine gun give it to that other bad cat, how come the FBI leave the back door open and them other two bad cats able to get out? Man, anybody know you gotta guard the back door when you got two bad cats up in a building and you know they got tommy guns too.

SHADDICK (*finishes the last slurp of his soda, pushes it aside*): Herman. There are multiple areas which I know nothing about. One is tommy guns, the other is bad cats, and still another is the FBI.

HERMAN: But they crazy not to guard the back door.

SHADDICK: Are they . . . yes, I agree. (*Waitress hands Shaddick a check.*) Thanks. . . . (*Points to Herman's soda.*) You finished?

HERMAN (*nods*): If it was me, man, I'd 'a guarded that back door—

SHADDICK: So we'll write to Hollywood and we'll put the question to them? Would that satisfy you?

HERMAN (*scratches his head, continues to sit there*): Maybe we gonna do that. I'll give you the words—what do they call that?

SHADDICK (*takes some money out of his pocket*): You'll dictate the letter.

HERMAN: Yeah, I think I gonna do that.

SHADDICK (*mumbles*): . . . back door. . . .

Shaddick pays the cashier. Herman moves past him, exits. Two Hoods approach Herman in the street.

HOOD ONE: Don't jus' stand there, baby . . . do a little soft shoe.

HOOD TWO: Yeah, boy, let's see you do it.

Shaddick comes out, stands alongside Herman. Hood Two sticks an unlit cigarette in his mouth, lounges against a car. He points at Shaddick.

HOOD TWO: Get a load of this . . . what a combination. Whadda ya say, Ike.

Shaddick, taking Herman's arm, starts to move down the sidewalk. The Hoods block his path.

SHADDICK: The name is Shaddick. (*Nods toward Herman.*) That name is Washington. What's the matter, cowboys? You bored . . . is that it? You got to go after an old man and a little boy . . . is that it?

HOOD ONE: I know who you are. . . . That's Moses. . . .

HOOD TWO: And this must be one of the children of the lost tribe of Israel.

Shaddick backs away to stand next to Herman. He looks warily from one to the other.

SHADDICK: You know who these are . . . two night crawlers in search of proof of manhood!

HOOD TWO: Manhood!

SHADDICK: Such courage, Herman; such courtesy.

At this point Hood Two advances on Shaddick, lashes out, pushing him against the wall, holding up one clenched fist as if to strike. Herman takes a knife out of his pocket and starts to run toward them. Hood One sticks out his foot, tripping Herman. The knife falls to the sidewalk.

HERMAN (*shouting*): Get the knife, Shaddick! Use the knife!

Herman moves toward the knife on his hands and knees, scrambling for it as Hood One pulls him back by the legs.

HERMAN (*screaming now*): Use the knife, Shaddick!

Suddenly the whole scene is engulfed in light as a police prowl car comes around corner—a spotlight aimed at them. The car pulls over. Two policemen get out.

COP: What's the trouble here?

HOOD ONE: No trouble, man . . . no trouble at all. We're just on our way out.

COP: Hold it. (*Moves over to Shaddick.*) Mr. Shaddick. You okay?

SHADDICK: In the pink.

COP (*to Hoods*): Take off.

Hoods get into the car, drive off.

COP: You want a ride home?

SHADDICK: My friend and I will walk.

Cop looks from one to the other, then suddenly sees the knife still on the sidewalk. He walks over to it, picks it up, closes the blade, then pops it open.

COP: Who belongs to this?
SHADDICK (*quickly*): That's mine.
COP: Yours?
SHADDICK: Definitely mine.
COP (*closes the blade again, moves over to Shaddick, hands it to him*): That's quite a weapon, Mr. Shaddick. Be careful with it. Give a yell if we're needed. Good night.

He turns, moves back into the police car, guns the engine. The car pulls away. Shaddick turns to look at the boy, then looks down at the knife in his hand. He hands it to Herman.

SHADDICK: Good night. (*Very softly.*) Put this in your pants and don't let me see it again.

The boy soberly takes the knife, looks at it briefly, puts it in his pants pocket. Then the two of them exchange a look.

SHADDICK: If it ever reaches a point where I must cut into another man's stomach, I will have lived too long.
HERMAN: Where have you been? You let some cat back you up against a wall and you don't do nothin' about it—you ain't gonna live long *enough!*
SHADDICK (*after a pause*): You'd have used it?
HERMAN (*nods*): If I had to.
SHADDICK (*looks off thoughtfully down the empty street*): Which is perhaps the worst thing about prejudice, Herman. The haters turn the victims into haters. You line up the two teams . . . and who's to tell them apart. (*Pause.*) So let's go home.

SCENE 4

The delicatessen, Herman and Shaddick enter.

SHADDICK (*with a look at the clock on the wall*): Look at the time. Past midnight. (*He locks the door.*) You got a toothbrush? All right . . . go.

Herman nods, moves toward the bedroom. Shaddick picks up an envelope.

SHADDICK: Herman . . . an invitation from Miss Ross for you to swim in the Country Club swimming pool. Reeking of perfume . . . and misplaced contrition.

Sticks the invitation under Herman's nose. Herman moves away.

HERMAN: You talkin' crazy again.
SHADDICK: Want to go swimming . . . shall we accept?
HERMAN: Yeah.
SHADDICK: Sure. . . . All right, go to bed now.

Herman moves into the bedroom. Shaddick follows him.

HERMAN: What you do before I come here?
SHADDICK: What did I do?
HERMAN: I mean . . . you never go fishing. You never go to the movies. You never drink no sodas.
SHADDICK (*looks off thoughtfully*): You know . . . you're right. This is the first movie I've seen since Myrna Loy. I used to love Myrna Loy. And I'd forgotten how good a soda could taste. (*Looks at the boy.*) At the risk of leaning on you, Herman—you seem to have opened up my life a little bit.
HERMAN (*very tightly*): You make a mistake if you lean on anybody. That what Bill say. He say never count on the other guy and don't ever turn your back. That what it all about.
SHADDICK: And if someone leans on you?
HERMAN (*very simply*): Break his arm.

Shaddick, after a long silence, walks over to Herman, looks deep into the boy's face.

SHADDICK: Listen, my little boychik—even if you think it— don't say it—all right? I have tasted more hate in my lifetime than I have wine.
HERMAN (*softly*): Man—don't you think I ain't?

Shaddick turns, goes through the partition into the other room, begins cleaning the coffeepot. After a moment the curtain parts a little, and the boy is standing there.

HERMAN: Shaddick? (*Shaddick turns to him.*) It don't make no difference—but you ain't chicken.

SHADDICK: I'm not?

HERMAN: No. You're a tiger.

SHADDICK: Then you tell me something. Why is my mouth dry and my heart still beating like it had been trying to get across the road ahead of me?

HERMAN (*with a little shrug*): You an *old* tiger.

SHADDICK (*with a smile*): Old tiger. . . . You remind me of that the next time I go crazy and think I'm Moshe Dayan.

HERMAN (*shakes his head*): Maybe you *ain't* crazy—but you *talk* crazy.

Shaddick waves him off, and he disappears into the curtained room again. Shaddick moves around the counter, pausing by the photograph of his son, looks at it.

SHADDICK: Good night, Benjy.

He takes a slow, shuffling walk to the stairway, flicks the light, and starts to move upstairs.

ACT THREE

SCENE 1

The Country Club dining room. The next day. Herman and Shaddick enter the dining room, sit down at a table, and look out the window.

SHADDICK: See Miss Ross?

A formidable dowager at another table calls over the Maître d', whispers to him. He casts a glance toward Shaddick, listens to the woman, and walks to Shaddick's table.

HERMAN: Next time I'm gonna go off that high board feet first. . . .

MAÎTRE D': Excuse me, sir. . . . I didn't see you come in.

SHADDICK: You're forgiven.

HERMAN: But I ain't gonna hold my nose or anything like that.

SHADDICK: He is available for Life Guard duties after lunch. Please inform the members.

MAÎTRE D' (*a little nervously*): The . . . ah . . . the pool and Club House are open only to members and guests.

SHADDICK: A fact?

MAÎTRE D': I'm afraid so.

SHADDICK: We are guests of a member.

MAÎTRE D': A member?

SHADDICK: Miss Gloria Ross.

MAÎTRE D': I see. Well . . . thank you very much.

SHADDICK (*to Herman*): Do you see anything you like?

Maître d' turns and moves back over to the table where the woman is staring at Shaddick and Herman with a cold imperious hostility. Then he turns back toward Shaddick.

MAÎTRE D': I wonder if I might have your name, sir.

SHADDICK: Shaddick. Abel Shaddick. And Herman D. Washington.

MAÎTRE D': I'll take your order in just a minute, sir.

The Maître d' nods and continues over to the woman's table. They speak in low voices. Shaddick studies this scene for a moment, then looks at Herman.

SHADDICK: Our enemies are multiplying, Herman.

HERMAN (*looks up, reading from the menu*): Hey, Shaddick—what's "ground steak garnished with delicacies, served in sizzling splendor"?

SHADDICK: Hamburger . . . overpriced! (*Again he looks toward the woman beyond them, who is staring at them with explicit displeasure. Shaddick leans over toward Herman, his voice lower.*) Herman—I got an idea! Let's go fishing at the lake. On the way is a diner where hamburgers are hamburgers and they cost a quarter.

HERMAN (*studies him for a moment, quickly looks toward the woman*): She's gettin' to you?

SHADDICK: I'm afraid we're getting to her.

HERMAN (*shrugs, rises*): I get my clothes from the locker. (*Herman exits.*)

Gloria enters from another room, moves toward Shaddick's table. Mrs. Parker approaches her.

MRS. PARKER: Gloria? (*Gloria stops.*) Are they your guests?

GLORIA: They're my guests.

MRS. PARKER: Well, my dear, I don't want to start anything. . . .

GLORIA: Then don't. (*She continues over to Shaddick's table.*)

SHADDICK: Ah . . . Miss Ross. . . .

GLORIA: How are you, Mr. Shaddick?

SHADDICK: Fine, thank you. And appreciative of the invitation. Herman enjoyed his swim—

GLORIA: You're not leaving?

SHADDICK (*with a look toward the woman beyond them*): We're going to the lake to fish. Here it is a little difficult to breathe.

MAÎTRE D'(*approaches Gloria*): Telephone call for you, Miss Ross . . . long-distance.

GLORIA: I'll be right there. Please wait—Please. . . . (*She goes to the telephone. Takes phone.*) Yes? (*She frowns.*) Who? I'm

119

afraid I don't hear you. Could you speak louder? Who? . . .
Mrs. Washington? Mrs. Washington—could you—could
you control yourself? I don't understand you. . . . That's
right. Please. . . . Now tell me that again, would you? . . .
(*Very softly.*) I see. I'm—I'm terribly sorry. Do you—do
you want us to tell the boy? . . . All right. Will you be
there the rest of the afternoon? I'll see that somebody gets
on the train with him back to New York. . . . Yes, I'll call
you later and tell you what train. That's all right. . . . And
Mrs. Washington—I'm—I'm truly very sorry.

*She puts the receiver down, walks across the room over to the
door where Shaddick is just about to walk out.*

GLORIA: Mr. Shaddick—that call was from Herman's grandmother.

SHADDICK: Oh. . . .

GLORIA (*a pause as she struggles a little*): It seems he had a
brother in Vietnam.

SHADDICK (*smiles*): You should hear Herman talk about that
brother! Lawrence of Arabia and Joe Louis rolled into one.

GLORIA (*softly*): He's dead, Mr. Shaddick. The grandmother just
received the telegram. He was killed on Monday.

*Shaddick stands there motionless. His eyes close for a moment.
His head goes down. Then he looks up, tears in his eyes. He nods,
gnaws on his lip, and just nods.*

SHADDICK (*turning to Gloria*): Who tells him?

GLORIA: His grandmother suggested that we do.

SHADDICK: We do? (*He takes a deep breath, closes his eyes
again.*) We do.

GLORIA: I . . . I don't know how.

SHADDICK: It's very easy. . . . You just stick a hole in the little
boy's heart and then you stand back and watch him bleed.

GLORIA (*her eyes glistening*): What can I do, Mr. Shaddick?

SHADDICK (*shrugs*): What can any of us do . . . (*He looks toward
the window.*) . . . except to start the bleeding process and
then . . . then hope that there's enough iron in that little
black frame to withstand the blow.

GLORIA: Are you going to tell him now?

SHADDICK: No . . . no . . . not here. (*They stand there waiting as Herman approaches.*)

Herman enters.

HERMAN (*to Gloria*): Thanks for letting me swim.

GLORIA: That's all right, Herman.

HERMAN (*to Shaddick*): You sick?

SHADDICK: No, Herman, I'm not sick.

HERMAN: We goin' to the lake now?

SHADDICK: Why not.

HERMAN: We gotta stop at the delicatessen and get the fishin' poles.

SHADDICK: If that's what you want.

HERMAN (*looks at him*): You sure you ain't sick?

SHADDICK: No . . . perhaps just a little.

GLORIA: I'll see you both later. . . .

Shaddick and Herman move toward the door. Herman carefully eyes her.

HERMAN: 'Bye. . . . She looks a little sick too.

The two of them move out of the room. Gloria stands there silently and motionlessly for a moment. Mrs. Parker rises, moves over to Gloria.

MRS. PARKER: Gloria, my dear—I don't want to make a thing about this—and this is hardly personal.

GLORIA (*in a soft, whispered voice*): Isn't it?

MRS. PARKER: There are certain lines that have to be drawn. I mean—to invite that old man—(*Gloria's face freezes, and it's the look on her face that stops Mrs. Parker cold.*)

GLORIA: That old man and that soon-to-be-ravaged, wounded little boy . . . are the only honest-to-God human beings within a radius of a hundred miles of this swimming pool. And that, Mrs. Parker, is meant to be extremely personal.

SCENE 2

At the lake. Herman and Shaddick are sitting on the rock, fishing. There's a dead silence—Herman engrossed in his fishing, Shaddick looking pale and old and waiting for the propitious moment. And finally, because he can wait no longer, he turns to the boy.

SHADDICK: Herman . . . I have something to tell you now. Something . . . something very serious.
HERMAN (*without looking at him*): What?
SHADDICK: Look at me, Herman. There was a call from your grandmother. It's about your brother Bill.

At this point the bobbin is suddenly grabbed by a fish and pulled under the water. It spirals down into the depths, carrying a fishing pole with it. Shaddick sits there alone looking after the running boy.

SCENE 3

The delicatessen. The bright afternoon has turned into a cloud-laced sky, darkening by the moment. Distant rolling thunder can be heard, and after a moment heavy splotches of rain fall. Shaddick walks slowly toward the delicatessen. Herman is standing by the front door. Shaddick moves to him, says nothing, just inserts the key in the lock, opens the door. Herman enters, walks the length of the counter, and disappears into the bedroom. Shaddick stands near the front door, then closes it. Shaddick pauses for a moment, then walks slowly over to the bedroom, stands at the curtains, then calls out.

SHADDICK (*calling*): Herman? May I come in?

There is a silence. Shaddick parts the curtains, moves into the bedroom. Herman has his suitcase on the bed and is thrusting in his belongings. Shaddick takes his suit off the hanger, lays it on the bed along with a shirt and tie. Distant thunder.

SHADDICK: The train leaves in about an hour. We have plenty of time.

Herman nods, finishes jamming the stuff into the laundry case, starts to close it, turns, looks up at Shaddick.

HERMAN: You know the fish?

SHADDICK: The enormous one.

HERMAN: You keep it. Eat it or sell it. I ain't gonna need it.

SHADDICK: What if I . . . what if I had it mounted? On a gold plaque? Your name on it?

HERMAN (*shakes his head*): Don't want it. I caught it for Bill.

With the articulation of the name, the cold steel defense of the boy is dented. He lets out one tiny, spasmodic sob that catches in his throat. Shaddick sits at the table, hands folded in front of him.

SHADDICK: If I said something, Herman . . . would you listen? (*Herman nods.*) A long time ago—almost twenty-five years ago—in this very room—I got a telegram. You know, Herman—the telegrams don't change. The wars change. The enemy changes. But the words used to tell the living about the dead . . . they don't change. . . . "We regret to inform you that your son, Second Lieutenant Benjamin Shaddick, was killed in action, June 14th, 1944, while on a bombing mission over Stuttgart, Germany." . . . I read that telegram, Herman, maybe a hundred times. I read it until the words seemed to float in the air in front of my eyes. (*He reaches across the bed to touch Herman's hand.*) Do you know what I thought then, Herman? I thought my life had ended. I thought there had been stripped from me some . . . some vital part of my body—that from that moment on I would never again be able to smile . . . to laugh . . . to enjoy anything on earth. I felt as you must feel now.

All of what the old man is saying does not reach Herman. But something of its truth and its understanding does reach him.

SHADDICK: You think at the time that the sorrow and the anguish is unbearable . . . and that the tears will never stop. But, Herman . . . the tears do stop. Somehow . . . some way . . . there is an end to the crying.

HERMAN (*very softly, pensively*): One time . . . long time ago . . . I jus' a li'l kid then. I got roller skates, see? And I start down the steps . . . and I fall. And man, it hurt real bad. And Bill come out and he go down the steps and he pick me up and he look at me and he say, "Hermie . . . Hermie—don't you cry." . . . I don't cry, Shaddick. Not me. I never gonna cry.

Shaddick rises from the bed, moves to the curtained partition, his back to the boy.

SHADDICK: You are a very brave boy, Herman. You are really incredibly brave. . . . You stay here—go on with your packing. I'll call you when it's time to go.

Shaddick comes out through the curtains, walks behind the counter, stops, his head down.

SHADDICK (*softly, under his breath*): Let this old Jew cry, Herman. I'll cry for the two of us.

Shaddick moves to the window. The rain now comes down almost torrentially, cascading against the glass pane. The tears roll down Shaddick's ancient, furrowed cheeks—much as the rain drops on the window. Herman comes out through the curtains, carrying his laundry case. He moves down near where Shaddick stands. Shaddick turns to him, wiping his face.

HERMAN: Why you cryin'? He ain't nothin' to you. You never even knew my brother. So why you cryin', man?
SHADDICK (*very softly*): I cry because I'm an old man, Herman. And sometimes . . . that's all that's left to old men. They cry at the irony of things. That the fine young men die . . . and the old men go on.

A car pulls up, stops. Gloria gets out, rushes through the rain to the front door, and enters.

GLORIA: I thought I'd drive Herman to New York, Mr. Shaddick.
SHADDICK (*looks at Herman*): It's for him to decide. The weather is so bad. . . .
GLORIA: It's begun to rain. I'll drive you, Herman. Is that all right?
HERMAN (*nods silently, stoically*): That's all right.
GLORIA: Herman . . . I'm truly sorry.

Herman again nods but says nothing.

SHADDICK: Do you want me to drive in with you, Herman?

Herman turns to him. There is a moment's pause.

HERMAN: No. No, you stay here. (*He picks up his laundry case.*) I ready.

Gloria opens the door, steps aside to let him pass. Herman moves to the door, then turns very slowly to look at Shaddick.

HERMAN (*very directly and with no emotion*): G'bye.

Shaddick takes a step toward the boy, wanting to say more, do more, show more, but he can't bring himself to try to scale the fortress that surrounds this kid. He puts his hand up in the way of a wave. Herman turns, follows Gloria out to the car. Shaddick moves back over to the window, just standing there.

Gloria and Herman enter the car. The engine starts. Then suddenly the passenger's door opens. Herman comes out, runs through the rain to the front door of the delicatessen, and then enters. Herman moves very close to the old man and looks up at him, then very slowly reaches up. Shaddick meets the hand and the two of them clasp.

HERMAN: I jus' wanna say somethin' to you—Don't you cry no more. Understand? We gonna make out. You'n me. We gonna make out—(*And then he starts to cry, and it's at this moment Shaddick takes the little boy to him, hugs him fiercely, protectively. Then very slowly they separate.*)

SHADDICK: When you come back, we can go fishing again.

HERMAN: I'm comin' back. I really gonna come back.

Herman turns, moves out the door and into the car. The car door closes and the car pulls away. Shaddick turns from the window, moves down the length of the counter, pausing—just to stand there, looking at nothing.

SHADDICK: Benjy. . . . (*The telephone rings. Shaddick turns, moves toward the phone, picks it up as if it weighed a ton.*) Yes? . . . Who? . . . A collect call. A collect call from who —I shouldn't ask. (*He closes his eyes, nods.*) Mr. Banner. All right; I'll take it.

A torrential outpouring of words is heard from the receiver. Shaddick simply stands there, shoulders bent, eyes half closed. He waits for the outpouring to dry up.

SHADDICK: Hello, Stanley. . . . What—I am sorry that the thing blew up. Yeah, you, you may come back and stay for as long as you want. (*Another outpouring of words. Then Shaddick looks up, studies the curtained room.*) No, not there. That room is reserved for Herman. . . . That's right —Herman Washington. He's a friend of mine. A very close and personal friend. That room will be saved for him. Upstairs, Stanley. . . . Think nothing of it, Stanley. 'Bye.

He replaces the receiver, looks briefly toward the curtained partition again, then takes a slow walk over to the counter and moves behind it to look down at the picture of his dead son.

SHADDICK: The dead, my son, come in all colors. You must know this. We, unfortunately, are still learning. (*He turns and looks down the length of the counter toward the window.*) It's raining quite hard, Benjy. A real summer storm. And this, I guess, will end the heat. End the heat . . . and cleanse the earth. (*A silence; he closes his eyes tightly.*) God, how we need it!

Then he moves down the length of the counter back to the window to look out at the falling rain.

Rod Serling

☐ At first there is a great deal of antagonism between Shaddick and Gloria Ross. Why do you think they dislike each other? How does their opinion of each other change? What causes this change?

☐ Shaddick tells Herman that the worst thing about prejudice is that "the haters turn the victims into haters." What do you think he means by this? How might this explain Herman's attitude and initial reaction to Shaddick?

☐ Where in the play do you think Herman first begins to change his feelings about Shaddick? Where does Shaddick first begin to open up to Herman? What do you think causes each one to change?

☐ What do Herman and Shaddick have in common that helps bring them together?

☐ How do you think Herman and Shaddick are changed by their relationship? What new directions might they pursue after this incident?

■ ■

■ After Herman had been home for a few weeks, he decided to write a letter to Shaddick. Compose the letter you think Herman may have written.

■ Perhaps you have seen this play on television. If not, imagine it as a stage or TV production. Write a review of the show as it would be written by a drama critic for a newspaper or magazine. This play records an imaginary experience. Discuss whether these characters and their world are believable and convincing. Mention what impact the show might have on an audience.

127

ABCDEFGHIJK 765432
PRINTED IN THE UNITED STATES OF AMERICA